He Restoreth My Soul

Book Three

May comfort and hope be attained by all who read

He Restoreth My Soul— Book One
Personal Stories of Sudden Loss

He Restoreth My Soul— Book Two
Personal Stories of Sudden Loss

He Restoreth My Soul— Book Three
Personal Stories of Sudden Loss

The Lord has blessed this project. We pray those blessings will be multiplied as the stories in these books are read and shared.

He Restoreth My Soul

BOOK THREE
Personal Stories of Sudden Loss

ANNA MARY ZIMMERMAN, EDITOR
ROY B. ZIMMERMAN, PUBLISHER

ROANN MENNONITE PUBLISHERS
22425 CR 42
Goshen, IN 46526-9215

He Restoreth My Soul—Book Three
Personal Stories of Sudden Loss

 Unless otherwise indicated, all Scripture quotations are from the King James Version of the Bible. The inclusion of poetry or prose with authorship unrecognized is unintentional.

ISBN: 0-9665661-3-0

ROANN MENNONITE PUBLISHERS
22425 CR 42
Goshen, IN 46526-9215

Carlisle Printing
WALNUT CREEK

2673 TR 421
Sugarcreek, OH 44681

Contents

The cross is for life;
the crown is for eternity.

—Roy B. Zimmerman

Preface

"...teach us to number our days, that we may apply our hearts unto wisdom. (Psalm 90:12)

God has called us into an "extended family" of those with whom we share a common bond: the sudden loss of our children.

Our first personal experience with such a loss was our firstborn son in 1971. We were brought to the depths of sorrow again when two of our daughters were called to eternity in a mini-van accident in 1987. After this loss, our friends began to encourage us to write our story. At that time it seemed near to impossible to write about our experience.

As the years went by, we met other parents who were grieving. Sharing with each other our painful journeys through the valley was beneficial in the healing of our wounded and broken spirits. The idea of a support group began to grow as we thought of the blessings it could bring to many.

For some time, we considered hosting a meeting for grieving parents. Then in 1991, our sister and brother-in-law lost a son in an accident. Now that idea of a meeting for grieving parents was revitalized, but still not realized. Another abrupt awakening came in 1995 when our granddaughter's life was snuffed out suddenly.

Now, we certainly wondered what the Lord would require of us. We decided it was time to move on with starting a support group. A committee planned a fellowship meeting in 1996 to which approximately one hundred families were invited. Each family was asked to send a short written account of their encounter with death and their healing experience. The plan was to put these stories together in printed form in time for the meeting. That plan was foiled as the lengthier stories came too late to be copied; some stories came in during and others after the meeting.

We did not feel right keeping these stories to ourselves. While we were considering what to do, the idea of a book was born. Stories continued to come in—enough to fill the pages of two books—and now three books.

Out of love, and with compassion for others, the families wanted to tell their stories. For in telling, there is healing. However, the *process* of telling is not easy. Personal notes included with many of the stories expressed that thought so vividly. One said, "This was *very difficult to write,* but if one sentence I wrote helps someone to the Christian walk of life, that would be wonderful."

One contributor expressed a concern that this book be uplifting. As parents who had lost a young son, they did not find it helpful to be reminded of the tragic circumstances of their loss. He wrote, "In our time of grief, it was not what we longed for . . . we needed to rise above calling it an awful tragedy and realize God had a plan for us." You may not yet find comfort in reading of the experiences of others—it may be too soon. If so, put the book aside for a while and come back to it later.

We trust *He Restoreth My Soul* will help many who are going through the process of healing. May the expectation of one contributor be fulfilled: "I eagerly look forward to a book where heart speaks to heart."

Other notes we received told of souls coming to the Lord at the time of the loss of loved ones. A recurring theme in the notes, and in the stories, is that of the sure hope we have of meeting our loved ones in Heaven.

One mother expressed it so well in their story: "We don't face a blank wall where we have no hope of being with our child again. Neither is it an open door for us to go through, but it is a window where we can catch the glimpses of glory awaiting us."

May we trust Him who is the source of all our hope and faith.

amz

Acknowledgments

Sincere heartfelt thanks to:

Families who spent countless hours writing,
then willingly contributed their stories.

Arlene Shaum for her original painting
which now graces the cover.

For He is our God;
and we are the people of his pasture,
and the sheep of his hand.
Today if ye will hear his voice,
harden not your heart.

Psalm 95:7, 8a

Nathanael Kyle Nolt

September 2, 1999 to May 15, 2002 (2 years)

Prepare To Meet Thy God

Doris Nolt, Mother

Our peaceful drive home from prayer meeting on Wednesday evening, May 15, 2002 was suddenly changed to an unforgettable experience in our lives. We never would have guessed that we had spent our last evening with our sweet two-year-old. Of course, later we said, "If only we had stayed home..." But we submit ourselves to the will of God and choose to rest in it. One lady told us "You will either swim or sink." We purposed by God's grace we would swim.

That day had started out as a fairly normal day. I remember having a conversation with Nathanael at lunchtime about heaven. Little did I know by the end of the day our son would be home with Jesus.

We spent the evening at prayer meeting. Just before dismissal time I gave our ten-week-old baby, Micaiah, to

Warren (Daddy) so I could hold Nathanael. He picked up a sheet of paper and amusingly placed it on my head. Quickly, I removed it. I gave him a hug and we looked into each other's eyes and smiled. That is my last sweet memory of Nathanael. I also recall him getting into the van when were ready to leave church.

After traveling several miles, we approached an intersection. The next thing I remember was hearing crashing sounds and wondering if Warren ran off the road and hit something. What was going on? A lady had run a stop sign, broadsided our van, and pushed us into someone's porch. The impact was incredible!

Warren, Douglas (7), Shawn (5) and I crawled out of the van. Zachary (9) was unconscious and was flown by Life Lion to Hershey Medical Center. He was hospitalized for six weeks due to a severe brain injury.

I lay down on the porch and Warren and the boys lay in the grass. While lying there I could hear baby Micaiah crying in his car seat. That was difficult! I felt I *had* to get him. A young girl who came on the accident scene crawled into the van, unbuckled Micaiah, and was able to quiet him. While lying there I heard someone say, "There's a little boy and he's not moving." Warren said to Douglas, "I believe Nathanael went to be with Jesus." Nathanael was killed instantly due to head trauma. The coroner said he did not suffer. That was a comforting thought to us. I'm grateful I did not see our precious little boy with such extensive injuries. I want to remember him with a happy, energetic body, and cheerful smile. I like the way a friend said, "One minute he was with his Mama in the van and the next minute with Jesus. Of course, heaven is ultimately where we want our children, he only went much sooner than we would have chosen.

The girl that caused the accident was taken to the hospital and released the next morning with only minor injuries. Warren, Douglas, and Shawn were taken to Good Samaritan Hospital. Warren was hospitalized for five days due to a shattered wrist and back injuries. Douglas wasn't hurt. Shawn had a broken elbow. The boys were released early the next morning and went to stay with friends. Micaiah and I were taken to Hershey Medical Center. Micaiah was kept for observation and released twelve hours later, uninjured. My youngest sister took a leave from her job, and she and her husband cared for Micaiah till I came home. Then they moved in with us for three months to help us. I was in intensive care for three weeks due to a ruptured spleen (which they removed), lacerated liver, bruised kidney, internal bleeding, broken ribs, back injury, collapsed lungs, and pneumonia. God so graciously spared my life, even though it looked doubtful at one point whether I would live.

Nathanael's funeral was planned to be held a week later in hopes that I could attend, but that wasn't possible. The undertaker so kindly brought the body to the hospital for me to view. Zachary was in a coma two-and-one-half weeks, so he never got to view. I remember the first thing I said upon seeing Nathanael was, "He's beautiful." How can this be true. Our very own son in his coffin. He had brought us so much joy! We so much wanted him in our family yet. What about all those unloved, unwanted two-year-olds — we loved and cherished our son. Again, we choose to trust our all-wise God. Praise the Lord for His grace and mercy, as my body needed all the energy it could spare for physical healing. Upon arrival at home, the house was full of reminders and memories. My grief started immediately. And oh, how very painful! A friend told me, "Just picture yourself in Jesus' arms and Him crying with you." That was a comforting thought. Douglas said, "I didn't want Nathanael to die. I wanted to teach him how to ride bike. His brothers missed him so much. Shawn and Nathanael had been such good playmates. Each of his brothers grieved, but in their own way. At bedtime Zachary would look real sad and say, "Nathanael." We knew he missed him. Due to his brain injury he could not express himself. He could not cry. Now nine-and-one-half months later, his talking is still limited and his right arm and hand hang helpless. He's back in first grade. His walking shows the most improvement. We take him for therapy three times each week.

Nathanael had enjoyed doing school papers when I schooled his brothers. His favorite toy was a play cell phone. He loved when I told him stories. His favorite song was, "He Was Nailed To The Cross For Me." At the end of the song he would say, "He was nailed to the cross for Daddy, Mommy..." and he would go on to name all his brothers. He is gone, but we never want to forget him. Our Comforter has promised we can see him again if we are faithful in our walk with God.

So much love and support was shown to us. We felt overwhelmed with gratitude. We could not have walked through this difficult valley alone. If you have supported us in anyway, we thank you at this time.

My friend had a vision of Nathanael. She said his face had a look of heavenly peace — a look of extreme happiness. She said it was a look you don't see on this earth. I treasure this.

Nathanael's last memory verse he learned was Amos 4:12, *"Prepare to meet thy God."* May it speak to the living. *"Even so Lord Jesus, come quickly."*

—Warren & Doris Nolt
Lititz, Pennsylvania

ANDREW LAMAR FREY

July 19, 1991 to October 2, 2000 (9 years)

"Watch Out!"

Raymond Frey, Father

Monday, October 2, 2000, the day started bright and early. We were going to try to seed 25 acres of wheat into soybean stubble. Calvin (11) and Andrew (9) had decided they wanted to disc the field before they go to school. So at 5:30 a.m. I awoke them to go discing. I told them that I would go get the tractor and disc ready. They put on their school clothes so they would be ready for school when they are done. My wife, Martha, sent a bag of chips along so they could snack. The last words they said were, "Good-bye, Mom. Bye, Dad," as they climbed into the cab of the tractor and left for the field. Martha and I went out to do the chores. Matthew (13) came out to help us a little later.

As we were walking to the house for breakfast, Matthew wondered whether he should take the truck out to the field to trade off with the younger boys so they could eat breakfast. I told Matthew that I needed the truck to get fertilizer at 8:10, so he should take the Kubota tractor to the field. We ate breakfast then fifteen-year-old Anthony left for work and Matthew went to the field.

When Matthew got to Calvin and Andrew, they were having lots of fun. They were both on the tractor seat. One would drive the one way down the field, then the other would drive back. As the one drove, the other ate chips. When Matthew got to them, they were all smiles, and teased Matthew with the chips because he didn't have any. Matthew pretended to be insulted by crying. They traded tractors so the younger boys could go eat breakfast. They waved to Matthew and started across the field.

When I went out the lane to get the fertilizer, I saw them coming across the field, never realizing that Andrew would never make it all the way in before the Lord called him home. The accident happened not more than two minutes after I left. When the boys came up to the cornfield headland, they started speeding up because it was nice and smooth. Alas! What they forgot was two washouts that formed through the summer because of heavy rains. Calvin was driving and Andrew was sitting on the fender of the Kubota with one arm around the roll bar and the other hand on the handhold used for climbing up onto the tractor. When they hit the first washout, the jolt sent the front end of the tractor into the air. Then Andrew saw the second washout and cried, "Watch out!" which were to be his last words. Andrew was thrown forward. He tried to hang on but the tractor pitched him right in front of the back wheel. When Calvin got the tractor stopped he ran back calling Andrew's name, but Andrew had gone to be with the Lord. Calvin raced to the house with the tractor.

He came into the house crying hysterically, "Andrew's dead! Andrew's dead!" His mother couldn't believe it but Calvin insisted, wanting to call for help. She felt numb, but told herself to stay calm. She called for the ambulance and they sent it on the road while asking directions. They also told her to try to get someone that could do CPR.

Martha called Leonard, my sister's husband, who lives across the road. He came immediately and drove back to the field. Not knowing where it had happened, he drove back to Matthew asking, "Where is Andrew?" Matthew didn't know anything had happened because where he was discing was downgrade from the accident scene. Leonard came back to the house, then left again taking Calvin with him. Upon finding Andrew, Leonard soon saw that life was gone. It seemed like a long time for Martha till the ambulance came, even if it was only about fifteen minutes. The police arrived almost at the same time.

With the fertilizer loaded, I headed for home, not realizing that anything had happened. As I was traveling down the side road close to our place, I could see neighbor Murray Bauman's pickup truck parked in our lane. Someone was standing beside it. As I came closer I could see that it wasn't Murray standing there. When I came closer to the lane, the shock hit me, as I could see flashers back in the field. I knew that something serious had happened. The feeling went through me that it could be that one of the boys fell off the tractor. As I drove in the lane, I could see then that the man by the pickup truck was another neighbor, Ervin Horst. He whispered to me, "It's Andrew." I jumped out of the pickup and ran over to the Kubota tractor. Driving back to the field, I met the ambulance leaving. I slowed down to talk to them but they motioned me to go on. I knew then that Andrew was gone because they were in no hurry.

When I got back there, I saw that my son was covered with a sheet. Martha came over to me and we cried in each other's arms. Calvin, Matthew, and my dad joined us and we all cried, clinging to each other. The policeman came over to talk with me, asking me if I want to go over and see Andrew. Leonard encouraged us to remember him as we saw him last, rather than as he was now.

We felt dazed and more or less did as we were told. We were very thankful for all the support from family, neighbors, and friends. The neighbors went ahead and planted the wheat, for I couldn't care less whether it got done or not.

Coming in from the field, it brought joy to our hearts to have our two little ones, three-year-old Timothy and one-year-old Rosalyn, run into our outstretched arms. There was now eight years' difference between Timothy and his next oldest brother. Timothy was ready to trade his teddy bear for Andrew — if only Jesus would!

Around 9:30 a.m. Anthony came home from work. It was a long ride home for him, all the time wondering which brother was killed.

The Grandmas soon arrived and took over the kitchen and the laundry. Among the first of the many people that came that day, was my brother-in-law, Paul Horst, a favorite uncle of the boys. It was good to see Calvin relax in his uncle's arms... Paul held him for a while.

While folding wash, my sister Karen asked, "Whose socks are these?" Matthew got up from his chair, grabbed the socks and put them into the garbage. She got the message. Obviously, they were Andrew's socks.

The next days were as if this just couldn't be true, yet we knew it was as we stood beside the coffin with our son, Andrew, in it. Many people came to share our grief and show their support. The day of the funeral came and we knew that this would be the last time we would see our son. We knew that we had to go on and that Andrew was in a better place than we were. But oh, the pain — for one of our precious children was gone! I still vividly remember how I felt the evening of the funeral after everyone had gone home. I said to my dad, "It just seems as if we are left all alone." Dad wondered whether they should come home with us. I said that they wouldn't have to. We knew that just because we were not surrounded with people doesn't mean that we were not surrounded with prayer. As I was doing chores that night, the tears just flowed as I cried to the Lord for strength to face each day, and that I could meet the needs of my wife and children.

What I missed most was Andrew's presence in the barn after school. He was always the first one outside to see what I was doing. He was very willing to do what we would ask of him.

We, as a family, can say that the Lord truly was faithful in helping us through the stages of grief. Many friends, family, and neighbors helped in making the load lighter. May we never forget what they have done for us.

—Raymond & Martha Frey
Newton, Ontario, Canada

ADRON JOEL ZIMMERMAN
July 25, 1994 to September 6, 2000 (6 years)

God's Grace Is Sufficient
Elsie Zimmerman, Mother

Adron was our third child. He was a friendly boy who loved people. He enjoyed hugs, puzzles, playing dolls or school with Emily, his older sister, or doing whatever his older brother Benjamin might be doing. We had five children. Their ages were as follows: Emily (9), Benjamin (7), Adron (6), Aaron (3), and Ethan (16 months).

Benjamin had just started first grade at school. Adron was eager for the time when he would also start school. He was in kindergarten at home and was doing some reading in a first grade reader.

On Labor Day weekend we had traveled to Ohio to be with family at a hunting cabin. The children had a wonderful time of riding four-wheelers over the trails, looking for deer and playing with cousins. We will always cherish this time together. It was the Wednesday after we came home from vacation that Adron was killed.

Adron had spent the morning doing dishes while I was working in the garden. He hollered out the window to tell me he will hurry with the dishes so that he can come help in the garden. After awhile Adron and his younger brother, Aaron, came and helped take off squash and tomatoes.

At lunchtime Kermit came home from work, sick with a headache and an upset stomach. He would just fall asleep while working at the computer. Any medicine Kermit took didn't seem to help. He went to lie down for a nap, hoping to feel better.

After putting the two youngest boys down for naps, I woke Kermit to tell him I was going to school to pick up Emily and Benjamin. When Adron came in from the sandbox I asked him if he wanted to go with me.

On the way to school we stopped at an intersection to make a turn. Adron asked, "What if we could get to the corner in a second?" At the time it seemed to be an insignificant question. But later as I reflected on it I thought of how his transition from here to heaven was just as quick.

Normally when Kermit came home from work he would stop at the mailbox. Because Kermit was already at home I thought we would get the mail.

Adron was sitting in the front seat. I parked at the end of our long lane and asked him, "Do you want to get the mail?"

"Sure!" he replied.

There was traffic coming and as I watched him in the rear-view mirror I saw he was looking intently down the road. Suddenly I was filled with apprehension. What if he doesn't look both directions? Maybe I should call out the window and remind him to look both ways, but knowing they had been taught how to cross a road, I decided not to.

After a dump truck went by Adron dashed across the road. I saw an SUV make a quick dodge and heard a thud. I cried out and ran to where Adron was laying on the road. I knelt beside him and cried out to God.

Such pain! It felt like a giant hand was squeezing the life from me, and I was overcome with guilt. Oh, why didn't I remind him to look carefully? Later, someone who had passed by just before he was hit told us that they had noticed the little boy standing there and he was looking both ways.

A man came up to me and told me not to move him. He asked his name. We called to Adron, but there was no response, and we could not find a pulse.

Emily and Benjamin ran into the house and woke up Kermit with, "Dad, Adron got hit on the road! We think he was killed!"

A man asked if there was something they could do. I told them to take the van up to the house and get my husband who was sleeping. He drove the van up to the house. The neighbor man came in and brought Kermit and the children out to the scene of the accident.

By that time the first responders were there and the ambulance came soon after.

I went to the hospital with the ambulance. As the EMT did CPR on Adron, I heard them asking, "Is there any pulse?" The answer was always, "No."

A neighbor man brought Kermit to the hospital and sat with us there. His wife took our children to an aunt's house.

When Kermit came to the hospital they directed him to the chapel to wait. Kermit knew when they took him to the chapel that Adron had died, but we still hoped for life.

As we waited the chaplain talked with us and recited Psalm 23 to us. The doctor came and told us that Adron suffered multiple blunt-force injuries, and Adron was dead.

There was so much pain. It seemed as if God was so far away. Looking back we know that if it had not been for the grace of God we would have drowned in despair.

Friends from church came to the hospital to be with us. We went in to where Adron was and spent time with him there.

Then there were decisions to be made. Do we want to donate any organs? We had never considered this before but it seemed to be the right thing to do. If someone could have a better life because of Adron's death, that was what we wanted.

Many friends were at our house that evening. We were blessed with many kind deeds during and after the time of the funeral.

We have found in this time of loss that we can experience the peace of God only as we give God His sovereign right in our hearts. As a sovereign God, He is supreme and has the right to bring those things into our lives that He sees best for His honor and glory. We look forward to seeing Adron in heaven when our life on earth is over. Not only do we look forward to seeing Adron but also to see God and what He will do for His glory.

I recently came across a writing that says so well what we feel.

"Once we agree with God that we exist for His pleasure and His glory, we can accept whatever comes into our lives as part of His

sovereign will and purpose. We will not resent, resist or reject the 'hard things', but embrace them as friends, sovereignly designed by God to make us like Jesus and to bring glory to Himself."

—Nancy Leigh DeMoss

—Kermit & Elsie Zimmerman
Goshen, Indiana

Lawrence Newswanger

June 7, 1993 (Stillborn)

Lois Newswanger

July 11, 1999 to November 6, 2000 (16 months)

Her Last Good-Bye

Kathryn Newswanger, Mother

The summer of 1993 our family numbered six: Aaron and I, Edward (9), Arlene (6), Vera (5), and Esther (3).

Then on the morning of June 7 we were blessed with another boy, but were unprepared for the shock when he did not breathe. There had been no sign of trouble during the home birth. The doctor tried his best to revive him, but it was not the Lord's will. At the time I did not even care, but after a good sleep, thoughts came to be reality. And in my weakness I questioned why this had to be? My spirits sank low. I did not want to see other people's babies, etc. I battled with acceptance for more than two years. Finally I came to the place where I knew there was no other way, but to accept it. Then came a deep peace I could have had long before had I only given up my own will. Yet, I am thankful for that experience. It was a great help in what was yet to come.

On June 23, 1996, another healthy chubby baby boy joined us. We were thrilled to have another boy in the family. We named him Marlin.

Three more years passed by when another daughter, Lois, joined us on Sunday morning, July 11, 1999. Her three-year-old brother, Marlin, wondered where our baby lives. He thought she did not belong to us. Then he asked, "When will she go home?" That time came sooner than we thought.

When Lois was seven months old, I had finished bathing her and wrapped her in a white baby towel which had a hood in one corner. Seeing her with the hood on her head and snuggled in the towel, Marlin remarked, "Now she looks like baby Jesus!"

At one year of age Lois was crawling everywhere. One day we all sat down for lunch, then looked at each other, "Where is Lois?" One of us remembered seeing her crawling up the stairway. There we found her in the big girls' bedroom playing with a blue stamping pad, with blue marks all over her face!

At fourteen months, Lois started walking. Now she often joined us in the barn for the evening milking. If she managed to catch a kitty she would squeeze it for all she was worth. She also loved to ride in the feed cart while her dad pushed it along feeding the cows. She, too, threw out handfuls of feed, but would never touch a cow.

Whenever we sang, Lois would sing too. The only words she knew were, "Happy Birthday To You". Big brother

Edward would tease her, and how she loved it. One day he sat on the couch reading a book. Lois came with her little plastic chair, set it in front of Edward, got herself a book, and sat facing him — little sister — like big brother.

When her big sisters, Arlene, Vera, and Esther went back to school I was kept busy running after four-year-old Marlin and fifteen-month-old Lois. We had beautiful fall weather so they were often outdoors. One day Lois wandered in to a pen with a newborn calf. I heard the calf's mad bawling and went out to investigate. Marlin came running and said, "Lois is under the calf." I ran... There she was flat on her back, unhurt, with the calf jumping over her. Lois' time was not up yet...

Sunday, October 29, 2000, was the last time Lois was at church. We had communion so her big sisters had her in the anteroom while we church members washed one another's feet. There were more babies in the anteroom and Lois gave each one a hug. Was it her last good-bye?

Sunday, November 5, 2000, we stayed at home all day. In the afternoon we were playing games around the table. Lois was in our midst, grabbing cards too.

Monday morning when I came in from the barn, Arlene (13) handed Lois to me while saying, "She has been fussy all morning." So I dressed Lois, and we all ate breakfast. Afterward I sat her on the big rocking chair beside the cookstove. I gave her a doll and her sip-cup with milk in it. She let her doll have a sip too. The rest of the morning Lois went with me wherever I went. She was not content otherwise. I put her to bed for a nap. She rarely took a forenoon nap anymore. She awoke in time for our late lunch.

After lunch we had chickens to dress for an Asian customer. I usually kept Lois with us, but it was such a nice day and she was happy, so I dressed her in her cap and coat and let her run with Marlin. After a while she came out of the kitchen to the washhouse where we were working. She went down on her knees to back out the next door and down one step to our backyard. But she hit the door frame and scraped her knee. I helped our crying girl to her feet and held her hand to comfort her, all the while dipping chickens with my other hand. I let go of her hand to get the next chickens, but she remained in the same spot. As soon as my hand was free, she held out her hand again. We held hands till she was ready to go. A little later she walked through the yard, past the open door with a paint tube in each hand. Oh, no, I thought. Marlin must be painting as Lois could not reach them. I checked, but he was all by himself in the barnyard.

Back at work, we had been visiting awhile when we thought we had better check on Lois. I went out the opposite direction from where I had last seen her going. Why? I don't know. I went all around the house, past the water garden, but I didn't stop to look in. I always checked there first, but an unseen force led me on and then back past the pond again. Now I searched farther, though Lois rarely went as far as the barn alone. I met our feed salesman and told him where to find my husband. I continued my search around the barn, and planned to look one more place. Then Aaron called and said he had found Lois floating on the water garden. He quickly phoned for help. I ran to the water garden. There I found our feed salesman doing CPR on Lois.

Advanced Life Support was in the area on another call, and arrived at our house within minutes. They checked for a heartbeat, etc. One attendant kept repeating, "She's so cold." The ambulance arrived, but there was no response from Lois. I was asked what we would like them to do. We didn't know. I am not good at making quick decisions, so they called a doctor and explained the situation. He suggested they stop all efforts to revive her. I felt comfortable with their decision. They laid her on the couch, where it appeared she was only sleeping. Her last bottle of milk stood on the back of the couch. We had Lois with us for several more hours till the undertaker came.

God had closed the book of her life. From experience I knew in my heart, I would be able to bear it by accepting it and knowing God had a purpose in this, that it was His will. Keeping my mind filled with these positive thoughts was a great help in the following days. My heart was filled with love for our petite little girl that was now safe with her Maker.

"To everything there is a season, and a time to every purpose under the heaven" (Ecclesiastes 3:1).

Much sympathy and support were shown to us by family, neighbors, and friends, known and unknown. It meant so much to our broken hearts, knowing others care.

My mother had shared with my sister of premonitions that she had that Lois would be taken from us several times before Lois died. But I'm glad she did not tell me beforehand. Yet it was a comfort knowing about it afterwards.

The autopsy report showed Lois went into shock as soon as she hit the cold water, shutting down her whole body, therefore no water had entered her lungs.

We know not what the future holds for us, but we want to follow where the Lord leads us. We can truly say our treasure is in heaven.

With the children's help we have written our own little book of memories. When we miss Lois we read the memory book. It cheers us up again.

—Aaron & Kathryn Newswanger
Narvon, Pennsylvania

Christian Martin

March 23, 1975 to June 10, 1999 (24 years)

Evan Shirk

December 8, 1972 to May 27, 2000 (27 years)

Our Season of Sorrow

Annetta Martin, Mother & Mother-In-Law

Yes, God does heal the broken in heart and binds up their wounds (Psalm 147:3).

We could not live long with such deep pain. It is four years since our son died. The pain does get less, but oh, how we miss him! I guess there will always be times, places and things that will remind us of those gone before. But we would not want to forget our loved ones. Precious memories, how they linger! We would not want to give up the valuable experience.

We are now new members of this group of travelers

who have trod the road of sorrow, and have met so many strangers who have become friends of ours. May God help us help others in their time of need.

Our sorrows began in April of 1999 when Roy's mother died of heart failure. She had not been well and longed to go, although she was only seventy-five years old. She lived in Pennsylvania so we were not used to having her around. We lived in Missouri and did not get to see her very often. Yes, it was still a shock to hear those sad words — *"Mother is gone."* For me, as a daughter-in-law, I never got real close to her as we moved away three years after we were married, but we all loved her. The house is so big and empty with only Dad there when we visit. He is now eighty years old and cares for his own house and dog. We thank God that he is well and on the go. Dad makes delicious chicken noodle soup, and other foods, which we have been privileged to partake of.

June 10, 1999 is a date which is stamped on our minds. Life has not been the same since. We look at everything a bit differently after seeing our son laid away. So suddenly, death came into our midst and snatched away one so full of life and energy. Christian — forever 24...

Oh, young people, turn to the Lord and let Him be your guide. Live for Him. He will ever help you make the right decisions and keep His protecting hand over you.

No, God does not promise us a life of ease without sorrow or pain, but He does promise us He will carry us through times of worry and woe. *"He will never leave thee, nor forsake thee" (Hebrews 13:5).*

We had no warning of the terrible day ahead. We all went to our jobs or appointed tasks. Oftentimes it was just Lee Edwin (15) and myself at home. Roy's job took him away from home several days at a time, but he was at home this

Thursday. He and Lee were working on our pickup truck. I thank God that He allowed Roy to be at home that day.

The day before, I had gone along to our Memphis, Missouri congregation for the funeral of our neighbor, Shannon Zimmerman's mother. Two van loads had met at Highpoint to shuffle the loads. When we got home in the evening, we were at Highpoint again when son Christian came by on his way home from work. He blew the horn and gave us a friendly wave out the window. With his silo-building job, he was often gone all week. We were surprised to see him coming home already. They had been working at Linn, Missouri, and were able to come home for the night. Home for the night — one last time.

How would we act if we knew tomorrow was our last day on this earth? Would we run here and there to make apologies, and asking for forgiveness? *"Take therefore no thought for the morrow; for the morrow shall take thought for the things of itself. Sufficient unto the day is the evil thereof." (Matthew 6:34).* Psalm 95:8 says, *"Today if you hear the voice of the Lord harden not your hearts."* Yes, make your things right today, for tomorrow may never come.

Thursday morning Christian left for work early. I didn't even realize he was leaving till I saw him going out the driveway — no time to say good-bye, or to wish him a good day.

God saw fit to take Christian from this life. It was his appointed time — no famous last words. If only we could have talked to him about — so many things — if only — if only!

That shocking phone call came saying that our son was in the hospital. It was a foreign-sounding doctor talking. I could not understand all he said, only that he was asking for Roy Martin. Roy was under the pickup and all greasy.

He told me to ask if he can call him back. So I returned to the phone, then the doctor made it clear that they have our son there. "Oh, which son? Is he yet alive?" Why did I ask that? With hesitation, he said, "I'm sorry to say, he is gone."

The silo they were building was already seventy feet high and they planned to go to eighty feet. All was going well until rain clouds appeared in the afternoon the sky. They quickly hurried to the ground to get under cover. Christian and his boss, Leroy Zimmerman, went down on the outside of the silo chute. They were on opposite sides of the chute, so they couldn't see each other. The other two workers, Earl Zimmerman and John Lehman, had already gone for shelter. So it was that no one saw what happened to Christian. Was he in too much of a hurry, then slipped and fell?

There was a veterinarian on the farm. He and the farmer were checking cattle. There had been two nets placed over the barnyard to provide shade for the cows. The veterinarian saw something fall between these two nets. From this perspective, it was estimated that Christian fell approximately 60 feet.

The veterinarian and the farmer quickly went and found Christian on the concrete. He was broken and life had already fled. They thought he might just be unconscious and tried to revive him.

The ambulance was called and Christian was taken to the hospital, but all efforts were in vain. His only injuries were a broken neck and leg and a cut above his eye. He might have died before he hit the ground. We have so many unanswered questions. This all took place mid-afternoon, and we got the call at 4:30.

Daughter Katie Mae was at home when the call came. She heard what I was saying and went for Roy. He took the phone and got more information. Can it be true — such shocking news?!

Roy asked our neighbor, nephew Wayne Shirk to take us to the hospital. The silo crew was there waiting on us in a room all by themselves. Also, Preacher Irvin and Emma Weaver came to be with us there. The doctor and two women came in to talk to us. It must be very hard to tell parents that nothing could be done to keep their son alive. How hard it must have been for the silo crew... There was nothing they could have done differently. It was Chris' appointed time — Thy will be done.

It was so hard to look on our son who was so full of life in the morning, and now so still and lifeless. He was naturally dark complected, but the sun had made his skin even darker.

Dear Lord forgive us poor, weak parents. It seems we may have failed somehow in helping our son to seek You — to be baptized...

Christian had his Bible by his bedside, so we trust he had been seeking. We hope and pray, *"Your grace was sufficient, and that he had time to say, 'Have mercy on me a sinner,' if he had not already done so." "For now we see through a glass, darkly; but then face to face: now I know in part; but then shall I know even as also I am known" (I Corinthians 13:12).* We'll understand it all by and by.

Coming back home — we never had such a sad day before. Family, friends, and neighbors there to give us support and consolation. We appreciated all the kind words of love and prayers. We were nearly overwhelmed with food, cards, letters, etc. It's never too late to send a card.

Our remaining family consisted of three sons: John Alvin (27), Wesley (18), Lee Edwin (15), and four daughters: Elizabeth (28) was living in Pennsylvania, Mary (26) married to Evan Shirk had two children, Martha (22),

Katie (20). Elizabeth did not get home until Saturday. Her friend, Elam, came with her as did others of the extended family. It surely was a long, hard trip for Elizabeth. Our granddaughter, twenty-one-month old Amanda, was so bewildered by all the sad people, she too wanted a handkerchief to blow her nose into. Grandson Jeffery at three-and-one-half months was more fussy.

Visitation was on Sunday at our church's community center. We were thankful for family-time before hand. Such a gathering we had never experienced before. We prayed and tried to sing, but how could we when we were so sad? There lay our son who was always on the go. Can it be true? "God is still on the throne, He loves and cares for His own..." That song comes to my mind often since it was sung at the Sudden Death Gathering at Buffalo, Missouri.

I felt numb and just went along with the decisions that were made by Roy and the children, with help from the ministry. The plans were made outside our house under the shade tree since our house was so small.

Around 1200 people went through the viewing line. Neither of the grandfathers were able to be there. My father, Christian Kilmer was just simply worn out, and we had expected to hear that he passed away, it was his namesake that passed away instead.

Grandfather Kilmer died two seeks later. I could hardly grieve for my own father. We felt sorry for my brothers and sisters who needed to travel from Pennsylvania twice in such a short time. We divided grandfather's earthly possessions on Monday following the funeral since the family was all there. (Mother had passed away the year before.)

We know not what the future holds, but we know who holds the future.

The following poem seemed to fit just right in our situation.

God's Flower Garden

Sometimes we can't quite understand
Our Great Creator's way.
When He takes a life so young
And leaves one withered, old, and gray
Whose life's work seems finished,
Perhaps waiting for the call.
While that life so young and tender
Held so much here for us all.

Then sometimes I get to thinking
Perhaps this world down her below
Is just a flower garden
Where God's flowers live and grow.
And perhaps when God is lonely,
Like us, He loves to roam
In His garden gathering flowers
Just to beautify His home.

Though He takes the full-blown flowers
Drooped and withered that need His care.
Still He needs a bud or blossom
To scatter with them here an there.
So He takes a few choice blossoms
Just the rarest He can find
And because God needs them up in heaven
Must comfort loved ones left behind.

—Poet Unknown

Yes, son Christian and Grandfather Christian died just two weeks apart. Could there be mix-ups in heaven? Did God's heavenly messengers take the wrong Christian? Now I need to learn to quit praying for Christian which I've just naturally done ever since he was born. I've learned to thank God that we had him as long as we did instead of omitting his name from my prayers. No, he was not more special than the rest. We could not have chosen which one should leave this earth first.

Sometimes I thought I heard Christian come in the door, or thought it was him when getting a glimpse of one of the other boys. One time Roy saw a man come across a parking lot, walking just like Chris — but no, it was a black man. At times we thought we heard his truck coming. Yes, there will always be reminders — even when we meet his friends.

The time came when we would be visiting with the boys and there was laughter. We needed to be joyful again. A person cannot bear such sharp pain and heartache for very long. *"Weeping may endure for a night, but joy cometh in the morning." (Psalm 30:5b).*

Only five weeks after Christian's death, my brother and his wife, John and Leora Kilmer, invited us to go with them to Ontario, Canada for the Sudden Death Gathering. We went along, but missed the first day because of van problems. Yes, we felt it very worthwhile to have been there — here were people who understood. Thinking of others was a great help in getting back to a more normal life. We needed to learn how to find a different pattern for our "new" normal.

On the way home from Canada we stopped at Jefferson City, Missouri, to see my brother Maynard in the hospital. He had cancer for two years and it seemed he was having more problems, but he looked good. We never expected him to answer the call only four weeks after Dad died on July 30, 1999. Maynard was sixty years old and left behind his wife and eight grown children, and some grandchildren. His passing made us appreciate each other more. Losing your other half must be so much more painful... Once again, all my brothers and sisters came to the funeral.

The owners of the farm where Christian's accident had happened were very touched by the tragic happening. They made a plaque to put on the silo in memory of Christian. We went to see them one year later, and just tried to imagine the horror of what they had experienced. Roy had helped build a silo on that farm years ago then a tornado wiped off most of the buildings.

Tragedy comes in different forms, and we were spared the horror of seeing him fall. Others have been right there when their loved one died, and possibly even felt they were the cause of death. May God help all those to forgive themselves and let His love and strength carry them.

The poem "Footprints In The Sand" means so much to us. We are sure God carried us through as there was no other way we could have made it.

Our son Wesley was nineteen that fall, and was baptized in November. Three days later he fell on the job while building a turkey barn.

He was on a beam which broke and he fell ten feet, landing on his back. He was sent to the second hospital because the first one didn't think they could handle his back injury. The x-rays showed a burst, fractured vertebra (second from the bottom), shattered into approximately fifty slivers. Wesley had hardly any pain after the second day. They put a brace on him and he laid flat on his back for seven weeks. Three days before Christmas he was allowed to get out of bed, but had to wear the brace for another five months. Roy stayed home those first seven weeks to be Wesley's nurse.

We all rejoiced when Wesley could be up and about again and praised God for granting healing. Were we given this trial to help us focus on something other than our grief? Yes, that first Christmas was a sad one, but we were glad to know Wesley was healing.

Once again we were abundantly showered with love and kind deeds. It was almost embarrassing to again be recipients of so much from family, friends, neighbors and strangers. *"For God loveth a cheerful giver." (II Corinthians 9:7b).* Not much is said about receiving. We were told that receivers need to be cheerful too, although it feels better to give. We tried to be grateful, but wondered if people didn't sometimes get tired of helping us.

In March, work began on our new house. We had talked for years about building someday, but never seriously. So some of our nephews went ahead and made plans... Many people gave of their time and some helped financially. In April Roy was working in the house on a scaffold over the basement stairway when he took a wrong step and fell down to the basement.

Preacher Irvin and Emma Weaver were here wiring the house, otherwise Roy would have been alone. Another trip to the hospital where Roy was told his wrists were both fractured. His plans for working on the house stopped. He thought it couldn't be... Yes, a person has to swallow their pride now and then. He had a cast on his right arm and his left arm was in a removable brace. He was still wearing the cast when we were once again reminded of how uncertain life is...

Saturday morning, May 27, 2000, we had preparatory services at church. In the afternoon our son-in-law, Evan

Shirk, received a summons on his pager to go fight a fire. He took the fire truck out alone. That was very unusual as they always waited on another fireman to go with them. It was a false alarm.

On the way back to the fire station, Evan somehow dropped a wheel off the edge of the road and the truck hit a culvert. It rolled and Evan was thrown out. His death was instant due to a broken neck. Others from the fire department were right behind him and saw it all happen. The truck caught fire and they thought he was still inside. They couldn't get to him from one side, so ran to the other side where they found him laying on the ground.

God needed *another* bright blossom, as the poet wrote, to brighten his home. But, oh, the anguish of the loved ones left behind — our daughter Mary and two little children, Amanda Joy (two-and-one-half years) and Jeffery Dale (one year), and another one to be born in November.

We were at home when the call came. I was making supper for Bishop Abner and Verna Oberholtzer. We dropped everything and Abners took Roy and I to Mary. We stayed there for the night and didn't go to church on Sunday for communion. Oh, another time of sorrow. We felt so helpless, trying to comfort Mary when our hearts were so heavy, so sad. This was almost harder, to see a daughter go through such sorrow, than to lose a son!

Our daughter Martha went to live with Mary. Martha taught school so she was gone days. After all, night time was the worst time for Mary. Roy and I stayed there at night too, and often in the daytime. Mary's friends were so good in sharing their time with her, and inviting her for meals, etc.

Memories of Evan

When I was a young girl we learned to sing a song
This little girl waited on her daddy so long
He was called so suddenly they couldn't say good-by
Now we know just how she felt as in our hearts we cry.

For we have a little girl who's in those shoes today
She also lost her daddy in such a sudden way
She and her little brother can't understand why
For "Daddy's gone to heaven way up in the sky."

He used to be coming home at suppertime at night
These little ones ran to meet him, it was their hearts' delight
To have Daddy tussle, then rock them to sleep
Oh Father in heaven Thy arms around them keep!

We spent the last Sunday together at their home
We never dreamed the tragedy that so soon'd come
Daddy entertained the children by flying a kite
His children running after him in sunshine bright.

Please send your guardian angels around them each day
Comfort and soothe them and take the hurt away
Also protect their mama keep holding her hand
Bless her and guide her 'til we reach the promised land.

—Annetta Martin

So many sad days — but God carried us again. *"In everything give thanks, for this is the will of God in Christ Jesus concerning you." (II Thessalonians 5:18).*

When Chris died we tried to think of things we could

be thankful for, one was that he was not leaving a wife and children behind — now so soon we had that too! Yes, in the death of our son-in-law, we are thankful that it was death that caused the parting. So often one hears of husband and wife leaving for some other reason.

Please dear brothers and sisters of the faith, turn to God and let Him be your comforter and councilor. Don't let Satan lure you to the world and all its empty pleasures and promises! His grace is sufficient for all our needs.

Mary had her struggles. And for her to give birth six months after Evan died, was not easy. The midwife and her helper came to Mary's house November 12 and I was there to lend my support. Baby Evelyn Faith was prayed into this world in more fear and trembling on my part than my own babies had been, even though I always felt it was a stressful, but prayerful time. This time I felt so helpless, but God saw us through again — and again three months later when Mary was not well. Her heart and body just had too much stress, although the doctors said it wasn't stress.

She must have been born with a weak spot in her heart. They gave Mary medication which she might have to take for life. She also had panic attacks, which are not easy to get rid of. But with God all things are possible and we have seen a lot of good times too.

When Mary came home from the hospital we brought her and the children here to live with us in our new house. We were very thankful for more space.

Eventually, we moved a house trailer onto our backyard which is where Mary and the children live for the last two years.

March 3, 2001, daughter Elizabeth and Elam Martin were married in Pennsylvania. Yes, this was a happy occasion, but I believe it was the first wedding I ever cried at.

Such days just reminded me of those dear ones who are missing. What would they be doing now? No, we would not wish them back into this sinful world, but just hope to have the privilege to go and meet them in heaven. May God ever be with us and guide our footsteps in the paths He has laid.

December 7, 2002, we were blessed with another granddaughter, Sarah, born to Elam and Elizabeth. This grandchild is 1000 miles away, so we will not see her grow as we do Mary's three children just across the yard. We were able to be with baby Sarah and her parents for the first week — such precious jewels — how fragile they seem.

April 5, 2003, daughter Katie Mae and Ivan Keith Sloan were joined hands in marriage. They started housekeeping in Mary's house, which she rented out. May God keep His hands over them and guide them in all things.

—Roy and Annetta Martin
Latham, Missouri

DANIEL WEAVER

March 10, 1996 to June 5, 1997 (14 months)

I'll Come For It Someday

Erma Weaver, Mother

On that particular day, Thursday, June 5, 1997 we had special church services for some people from Virginia. There are several things about that day that stand out in my memory. One was how the visiting bishop touched on the subject of children: The faith of Naaman's wife's maid, and of how precious these little children are, and of the responsibility of parents to raise them for God.

We had a thunderstorm with wind that afternoon, which we feel was a factor in the accident. The cows were in the meadow when the storm came up and crowded in when the doors to the barn were opened. The steel grating over the reception pit was moved enough by the impatient cows to slip past its holding irons, but not enough to be noticed.

(Most people envision a pit as being outside a barn or

in a manure yard. This was a reception pit, two-by-two feet square, inside the barn and covered with steel grating. About twelve inches of grating is exposed from underneath the barn cleaner hood.)

It had cleared off to be a beautiful evening with bright sunshine and a gentle breeze. I decided to do some washing that evening, and remember taking in the beauty of the deep peace — how thankful I felt. The children were all healthy and the little ones played happily. The older children were going about their varied chores.

Daniel had been begging to go out. Lydia (10) was on her way to feed the cats and asked if she could take Daniel along on the wagon.

After the milking was done Noah picked Daniel up and started to bring him in, but noticed nine-year-old Alvin was having trouble feeding a newborn calf. With Noah's help the calf started drinking right away. Then he heard a rattle and recognized it as the steel grating. Alvin saw Daniel go down through the grate.

The barn cleaner hood is about four inches above the grate. The grate worked like a seesaw, flipping back into place after dumping Daniel in. Had there been no witnesses no one would have thought of looking there for Daniel. Noah grabbed a rope that was close by and removed the barn cleaner hood and the grate. He then tied the rope around his waist and fastened it to the gate of the pen beside the reception pit. He sent Alvin to get me and slid down the rope.

Noah found Daniel and wedged himself against the pit walls with his knees flexed against one wall and his shoulders on the other side with Daniel on top of him. Daniel cried when Noah cleaned his face. That made Noah feel so good, thinking, "I have him now. Now I'll wait till help comes."

I was outside when Alvin came running out of the barn. Seeing me he called, "Mom, you must come! Dad said so. Daniel fell in the pit! Dad went in to get him." Can you imagine what those words did to me? Unexplainable feelings! I ran, and at the same time thought of all I had ever heard of pit gas. I thought then that I would lose them both.

Alvin was about half the barn length in front of me and heard Noah. He called back to me, saying, "Dad said he has him." I heard Daniel give a little cry, like waking up from a dream. Kneeling at the edge of that black hole I called to Noah, "Should I call 911?" There was no response. All that could be heard was Noah's labored breathing. I tried to send the children to the house, and I ran for the barn phone. I called 911 and got an immediate answer. Running back I again called to Noah. There was no answer, nothing except that labored breathing.

Not long before this the firemen, etc., had come to school and talked about safety and had shown their equipment. Alvin had seen this demonstration, so he told me to get matches to burn the gas. Finding some in the utility room in the barn, I struck a match and held it down as far as I could while trying to look in. After striking the third match and not being able to see, I realized that 911 would be too late.

I ran for the phone when I thought of my brother-in-law, Johnny, a mile and a half away. When Marlene answered I almost shouted telling her, "Send Johnny over, Noah and Daniel are in the pit!"

Alvin asked, "What can we do? Dad can't breathe, I can hear it." Again I told the children to go to the house. I was so afraid someone would fall in. Tugging on the rope and holding tight, I could feel the immovable weight and heard the labored breathing. I began to call down to Noah, wishing he would answer, but his breathing was getting quieter.

The children came to the end of the breeze-way and called, "Johnny is almost here." By the time Johnny came running down the walkway, the pit was too quiet. That quietness was much worse than any sounds of labored breathing. Johnny and I pulled, but could only get him up part ways. Putting the rope over the gate bar, we tried again.

Johnny told me his brother Paul would soon be here, that we'll have to wait. With Paul's help we got Noah up to grate level, where he got caught again. Lowering him enough so that Johnny could turn him, we pulled him up.

Noah threw up right away, but was limp and unconscious. Johnny started cleaning his face. I heard him say that Noah was still breathing. The phone was ringing and I ran to answer. It was 911 to tell me they are on the way, asking if I still needed them. "Yes! PLEASE, my husband is out, my son is not." Only then did I think of Daniel. Running back to Noah, I told the children to stay in the house. "Go in and pray," I told them.

Paul was opening the barn doors while Johnny pulled Noah outside for fresh air. He was still limp and semi-conscious but had started responding.

The first thing he asked about was Daniel. I had to tell him that he was still down in the pit. As Noah was going into shock he said, "But I had him. He was in my arms." I asked for a blanket, but there was none because the ambulance wasn't there yet. I kept talking to him. He was covered with manure from head to foot and soaked from the shoulders down. Noah soon felt good enough to walk to the milk house.

I ran to the house for clean clothes for Noah while Johnny started to wash him with warm water. Coming out of the house, I met Marlene who had been brought over by the neighbor lady. She went into the house to stay with the children.

The ambulance, fire truck, etc., were arriving and roadblocks were set up. I was given a blanket. After Noah had changed clothes, we walked out to the scene again. They had a long handle with a hook. One man was fixing to put on a mask and tying a rope around himself. Then he asked Noah how deep it was, and hearing, "Eleven foot," they soon brought Daniel up. A medic attendant said, "We must at least try."

After the ambulance left we went into the house. Noah cleaned up and changed into his Sunday clothes, which he had so recently worn for church. I changed too, but dirty as I was, didn't clean up much. A neighbor took us to the hospital, where after a short wait, we were met by our family doctor. He told us that they got a slight heartbeat, but nothing they could work with or increase.

They told us if we want, they could fly him to Rochester to a bigger hospital with more equipment. We felt it was useless and the doctor agreed. He said, "We'll try a little longer." In a short time he was back, saying how sorry he was and that we could see him if we want.

What an experience — to hold a loved one for one last time.

The following poem was read at Daniel's funeral. We thought it was very fitting.

His Plant

One day the Great Gardener entrusted to me
A slip to be raised very carefully;
"I'll come for it someday," He said with a smile
So tenderly nurture and tend it, meanwhile.

I nourished it well, and the little plant grew
Till a blossom appeared of rich color and hue;
Its fragrance was like the aroma of spring,
And oh, what a delight to my heart it did bring.

Of all my plants this one seemed most rare—
So fragrant its blossom—so wondrously fair;

The desire to keep it within me did burn,
But the Gardener had carefully planned its return.

He presently came and He wanted to see
The slip of a plant He had once loaned to me;
I trembled and yet, had He not made it plain,
At some future time, He would want it again?
"It's perfect," He said, as He caught its sweet scent
Then softly He spoke as above it He bent;
"If left in this soil it will soon lose its bloom
I'll transplant it now in My garden at Home."

He tenderly lifted and bore it away
To bloom in His garden forever and aye;
And someday I'll see in that garden so fair
That flower that since has bloomed over there.

—Poet Unknown

Two-month-old Jason soon wore Daniel's clothes, so they were never put away. The clothing that Daniel had on when they pulled him out of the pit were never returned to us. He was barefoot at the time. Incidently, the shoes that fit him had been worn by his five older brothers, then worn by three younger brothers also.

We had two girls and five boys older than Daniel, and now there are one girl and three boys younger.

We cannot find words to express our thanks for all that was done for us. A mere thank-you seems so inadequate. We feel unworthy, but greatly appreciated it all.

—Noah & Erma Weaver
Orchard, Iowa

David Brubaker

November 1, 1992 to April 17, 1995 (2 years)

A Freak Happening

Esther Brubaker, Mother

Greetings to all who read of the experience we had on April 17, 1995. Even though eight years have passed since that day, memories linger on.

It was the first warm day that spring, and our two boys, Norman (4) and David (2), were playing outside most of the day. They went from playing in the sandbox to climbing around on the equipment — just anything little boys usually do. Leroy had been gone for the day. When he came home, he met the boys walking in from the field. When they passed the equipment shed, David wanted his dad to give him a ride on the tractor but they walked on without the ride. They went to the chicken house where David mysteriously bumped his head. A lump showed up later on.

A little later David's foot got caught in the corn head which was setting outside the equipment shed. His dad helped him get loose. David again asked his dad if he is going to drive the tractor, but no, Dad had other plans. David had such a strong desire to go on the tractor.

When suppertime came, everyone was in the house but David. (He usually played with his brothers and sisters and was not one to wander off alone.) I asked nine-year-old Jason to go look for David. Four-year-old Norman went along too. *I never thought how they would find him.*

They found David in the equipment shed, hanging by the hood of his jacket from the tractor. His head was hanging down and Jason thought he was sleeping. Jason worked hard to lift David's limp body so he could get his hood loose from the fender brace. David fell to the ground after Jason had him loose. We were thankful we were spared in seeing David hanging there.

Jason carried David's limp body to the house. The first glance of his off-colored face told me something unusual had happened. He was making an inhaling sound every so often. We tried CPR on him, but didn't have much success.

The ambulance was called and they got his heart beating again on the way to the hospital. At the hospital they decided he needs more oxygen to his brain, so he was life-flighted to a larger hospital. On the way to the larger hospital, I remember thinking I would rather see him go on than to have him come back to live as a vegetable.

They soon gave up on him as he was brain-dead. Actually, it was a relief to know, but hard to grasp. We tried to keep in mind that God makes no mistakes and He does not give us more than we are able to bear.

Friends and neighbors came to help get ready for the

funeral. What would we do if we had no friends? The many poems, letters, and cards that were sent to us afterward were a big help too.

The children adjusted well to their brother's death. One brother said, "David was cute. I wish he wouldn't have died." Yes, he was a cute angel. He was always our shy little boy. Other people didn't see him smile very often, but at home he was like any other child.

Later, Leroy asked Norman why they were walking in the field that day. He said, "David said, 'Vise, vise (white)'," and walked toward the field, but Norman didn't see anything white. It does make us wonder, *"What did he see?"*

We are thankful for all the precious memories we have of David. We would not wish him back into this sinful world since we know he is at a much better home.

This experience was a stepping stone for us. We would rather part with an innocent child than to see one of our children choose the ways of the world.

We would not long for heaven if earth held only joy.

—Leroy & Esther Brubaker
Withee, Wisconsin

Lucetta Ann Weaver

July 18, 1988 to August 2, 1990 (2 years)

She Is Gone

Julie Weaver, Mother

Thursday, August 2, 1990, started out like normal on our Fairview, Michigan dairy farm. Our seven children kept life lively and they also helped a lot with the work. Hannah was 14, Titus (11), Ammon (10), Eunice (8), Laona (6), Joel (3), and Lucetta (2).

Lucetta was with Joel everywhere he went. She loved to be with her daddy also. When he would come into the house she would run and hug him around the legs.

At that time Mike was chopping feed several miles from home and would bring it home to feed to the cows. This iwas about the only time he took Joel and Lucetta with him. The Allis tractor had a half cab. Lucetta stood on the seat and Mike could feel her feet under him as he sat. Joel stood beside him. Lucetta kissed Eunice and waved good-bye as they left on the tractor with Mike. I was making apple sauce while Hannah cut hay.

Following is Mike's story about what happened after he got to the barley field.

I was getting on the tractor after hooking up the chopper and wagon. Lucetta stepped off the seat onto the right side where the hydraulic controls are. Joel climbed on the seat. Usually I made Lucetta stand on the seat. I don't know why I let her stand there beside me. I guess I thought she would be safe on that side because the bottom of the cab came to under her shoulders. I chopped one round with my arm around her. I still can see her looking into my face smiling, and then looking back watching the feed fly. As I came to the end of the field I shut the chopper off and went back into the wagon to level the feed off. I thought I'll chop just a little more. I turned to the left using my right hand to put it in gear. I don't know where my mind was, but I don't remember much until Joel tapped me on the shoulder and said, "Lucetta". I turned to my right and she was gone.

Quickly stopping and looking back, I saw her lying on the ground twenty to thirty feet behind the wagon. I jumped off that tractor and ran to her saying, "Lucetta, you have to be all right."

As I got closer and saw how still she lay, I thought maybe she was unconscious. Lucetta did not move. I picked her up and knew she was gone. The Lord had taken her before I got there. I cried, "My dear Lucetta," kissed her and laid her on my shoulder. I ran for the tractor and drove as fast as I could to my brother's house nearby. As I left the field the words of the song, "God's Way is Best" came into my mind.

Back at our house, my sister-in-law, Marlene, called me and said that Mike had a mishap with Lucetta and that I should come quickly. As I drove up to Marlene's, Mike was running out of the house with Lucetta. They were both bloody so I knew it was bad. I asked Mike how bad she was, and he said, "She is gone."

Marlene had called the doctor's office. Mike got in the van and I drove. We cried and talked on the way to the doctor's office. I told Mike that I don't blame him. How could I? He loved Lucetta so much, and I loved him. They told us she had died instantly of massive head injuries because of the feeder wagon going over her head. We asked if we could take her to the funeral home. We were given that opportunity.

I held Lucetta at the funeral home while we talked with the director. Then we laid her on a steel table and looked at caskets. Before leaving we went and kissed her and came home alone. Our baby was there on the steel table, but in reality she was in heaven with God. What a blessed thought amidst our heartbreaking grief.

People came that same day yet bringing food, helping with the hay, and doing chores. What would we do without family, friends, and our church people?

We had the viewing in our home. This proved to be a blessing to us to have her body with us. It was something not normally done in our community.

Lucetta died on Thursday and the funeral was on Sunday afternoon. After that the Thursday of every week was a difficult day for a while. Later, the second day of every month was a reminder of her death. All the "firsts" that year were hard to cope with. Several months after her death someone in the community sent a sympathy card telling us they are still thinking of us. That meant so much to us. After a while we felt like everyone had forgotten our hurt. Especially in the first year after her death, we needed to be reminded of people's love and care, and that they hadn't forgotten us.

Time does pass, and now it has been thirteen years since Lucetta is gone. We moved to Wisconsin and had two more sons.

What have we learned through this experience? Life is short for some. Each one needs to be ready for death. If we feel guilt at what has happened, we need to lay that down at Jesus' feet and go on. Heaven is dearer with a loved one there. It's never too late to send a sympathy card. God is all-knowing and all-powerful. He is in control of everything. This has been an experience we wouldn't have asked for, but one we wouldn't have wanted to miss.

—Mike & Julie Weaver
Withee, Wisconsin

God's Way Is Best

God's way is best; if human wisdom
A fairer way may seem to show,
'Tis only that our earth dimmed vision
The truth can never clearly know.

He leadeth true; I will not question,
Tho' thro' the valley I shall go,
Tho' I should pass thro' clouds of trial,
And drink the cup of human woe.

Chorus:
God's way is best, I will not murmur,
Although the end I may not see;
Where'er He leads I'll meekly follow—
God's way is best, is best for me.

—Excerpts from 389 in the *Christian Hymnal*

Leon David Zimmerman

January 18, 1986 to August 5, 1987 (18 months)

God's Rosebud

Esther Zimmerman, Mother

August 5 dawned with a hazy, hot summer sky. The few days before had been one hundred degrees or higher and it seemed this day was going to follow suit.

My husband, Melvin, milked forty cows along with farming and hay-making on another farm for a blind man. We also lived on a farm so he was a very busy man, managing two farms. I helped the best I could.

On this particular day, the morning began as usual. I made breakfast for Melvin at 5:30. I, being a lazy person, then crawled back into bed for a little snooze till our children awoke.

After dressing little eighteen-month-old Leon, I gave him and four-year-old Lisa breakfast. Really, Leon wasn't very little and people often commented on how big and robust he was.

I can't remember what all the children did that morning, but I do remember Leon took some toys from his sister. He was getting to be very independent, and at times we hardly knew how to discipline him. But I have precious memories of that morning. After giving Lisa's toys back and spanking him, I held him and tried to explain why he should not take other people's toys. What a pleasant surprise? He seemed to understand and relaxed on my lap. He seemed reluctant to get off my lap to play again. Was Leon trying to tell me this would be my last chance to hold him? Little did I know, or I would have been very reluctant to put him down. I have often been so thankful God granted me the opportunity to hold him one last time that morning before he died.

After giving the children each a pretzel, they went outside on the porch swing while watching the traffic pass by. One of the trucks that passed was the children's Uncle Leroy Zimmerman with his driver and crew. Leroy was a silo builder and I assumed he was headed out-of-state for the week. I remember Lisa told me Leroy waved to them. Little did he know that he would have to leave his job site early to come home for his nephew's funeral.

About 10:00 a.m. I sat down to right a letter to a friend. After awhile the children wandered off the porch and around to the back of the house.

The evening before we had bush-hogged the tall weeds around our hog lagoon. Since the children had never made any trouble going to the lagoon, I wasn't worried that they would go there now.

I could hear their childish chatter while they were playing in back of the house. Thus, I got involved with my letter writing in order to beat the mailman.

After a while Lisa came in all excited, saying, "Leon is

splashing water. Leon is splashing water."

It seemed there were two forces working within me, one telling me to run and look now, the other kept me at the desk writing my letter. I know now it was God who kept me there. He wanted a rosebud in heaven.

I reassured Lisa that I would go look as soon as I sealed and mailed my letter. That only took three or four minutes. I was not too worried because we had a five-gallon bucket in the horse's stall which Leon often splashed in while reaching through the guard rails on the outside of the stall. I felt sure that was where I would find him.

After walking to the mailbox with Lisa and mailing my letter, I went with Lisa to the barn in search of Leon. By now she seemed to have forgotten about it, or at least was not so excited. After not finding Leon in the barn, I still wasn't too worried. One other time he had wandered a little ways into our forty-acre corn field. After I had called his name, he cried and I easily found him. So I thought that was probably where I would find him this time.

I called his name as I walked by the corn field on my way to the lagoon — no Leon. That was when I became frantic. I ran through the first few rows of corn calling his name, then on to the soybean field. A neighbor said he passed while I was searching the soybean field. He thought he should stop to see if he could help, but something made him go on.

After searching for fifteen minutes, I returned to the house and prayed and cried. Something told me Leon was in heaven. Oh, it was hard, surely not — surely he was alive and lost in the corn field. Then all of a sudden I felt much calmer. I remember looking at the clock. It was 10:30 a.m. Then I called a neighbor lady and asked her to please tell Melvin to come home because I couldn't find Leon.

A very concerned neighbor lady brought Melvin home and helped us search for a little while. But since it was a very humid day, and her being older and used to air conditioning, we told her to go home.

We soon saw we needed more help. We had very nice neighbors on whom we called to help search the corn fields. I don't remember how long we searched till we decided to call the rescue squad.

I had just gone to the house for a refreshing drink of water and a chance to get out of the hot sun when I heard the cry, "We found him. We found him."

I ran out the back door in anticipation of holding my dear lost son. But, no, the still form my husband was carrying was my son, though not alive.

There under the shade of the spreading elm tree I held my precious son for the last time while my tears flowed unending. *How could this have happened to us? Why, Lord? Why? Why did it not happen to someone who didn't want their child anyway? Why us? We loved him so. And then came the battle of guilt I so often fought, even months later. Why wasn't I a better Mother? Why didn't I check on him sooner?*

This happened on a Wednesday afternoon. We had searched a total of three hours till Melvin happened to see Leon's body floating atop our lagoon. We had looked there often, but had not see him. It wasn't long at all till the rescue squad came. They pronounced Leon dead, then took his body by ambulance to the funeral home.

A kind neighbor lady who had come to help search offered to take us to the funeral home to make arrangements.

The funeral was on Saturday forenoon. We lived across the road from the church house, so we did not need a hearse. We had only two pall bearers. One was Leon's uncle, the other his second cousin. It all did not seem real with lots of travelers around, etc. But reality hit after they all left. How quiet the house was. Lisa asked so many questions that were so hard to answer.

Time is a great healer. The prayers said on our behalf, and all the kindness, food, and love shown to us sure made our grieving a lot easier. We felt so unworthy of it all. We received over three hundred cards and letters up to a year later which really meant a lot to us, especially from those whom had similar experiences. We, in our weakness, want to try and remember others in time of grief.

It is now going on seventeen years since we lost our dear son. Time is a great healer, and now only fond memories remain. We wonder sometimes how life would be were he still living. Possibly, Melvin would have been a big help to us, but we would not wish him back. We are thankful he was spared from all the trials in this life.

Those first few months after Leon's death, family gatherings and seeing others his age were all so painful. I remember just the Sunday evening before he died, the family was all gathered at Melvin's parents' house. Each family was given a pork roll. All the rolls were on top of the sink. Well, Leon was a climber and into everything. He climbed on top of the sink and took a bite out of one of the rolls. My sister-in-law later said she got that roll and had pleasant memories whenever she saw his teeth marks.

Since Leon's death we have had four more children. The first two were girls. We thought maybe God wouldn't grant us another boy — later we were blessed with two more boys.

We miss Leon, but he is safe in the arms of Jesus. We would not wish him back.

In Loving Memory of Leon David Zimmerman

One long year has now passed,
Since we lost our dear son.
But sweet memories of him still last,
From the dawn till setting sun.

For many are the times remembered,
Of the way he used to smile.
The many ways he helped to brighten,
And make our life seem more worthwhile.

His pitter-pattering feet no more
On our kitchen floor shall walk.
Oh how our hearts for him do ache,
To hear his laughter, and baby talk.

Lisa, his dear earthly sister,
How she missed him those first months.
Many were the questions, answers,
"Where is Leon? Above the sun?"
Tho' he'll always be remembered
Sadly missed by all, we know,
Yet we'd be oh so selfish,
To wish him back down here below.

For we know our Leon is happy
When with God's angels he does play.
Thus we do not want to question
God's almighty — all-wise way.

—the family

—Melvin & Esther Zimmerman
Versailles, Missouri

Edwin Lamar Burkholder

December 29, 1969 to October 13, 1973 (3 years)

An Unforgettable Weekend

Floretta (Flossie) Burkholder, Mother

Friday, October 12, 1973, Ammon and I and our three-year-old son Edwin left our home in Pennsylvania and traveled to Ohio to visit my sister's family, Sam and Mabel Leid and their daughter Lillian, who was also three years old. My parents, Frank and Reba Martin, my youngest sister Julia, and brother Harold's wife and family also went along. We began our trip at 9:00 p.m. so that we would have all day Saturday to visit with my sister. Little did we know what lay ahead for us. The memories are all very clear even though the wound has healed. Time has a way of doing just that, with the Lord's help.

We got to Mabel's place at 7:00 a.m. It was a nice day so Lillian and Edwin went right to playing outside. At 10:00, I went to make sure they were all right. It seemed they were playing nicely. About fifteen minutes later Lillian came in and said that Edwin was in the water. I ran out right away, but didn't know where to look. My mother heard water splashing and found Edwin in the well. The men were helping Sam, my brother-in-law, bring hay to his farm from a neighboring farm so they were not there at the time. We women didn't know what to do, or how to get Edwin out of the well. When the men drove in, I ran partly out the lane and told my husband Ammon what happened. (Anyone that has an experience like this knows the anxiety that goes with it, and also the prayers that are sent heavenward.) We put a rope around Sam's waist. The men held the rope so he could go in and get Edwin out.

By this time my sister had called her neighbor, Mrs. Bob (Mary) Dawson. Mary called the rescue squad. Almost all the neighbors arrived the same time as the ambulance did. The ambulance crew tried CPR, but couldn't get a response. They decided to take Edwin to the hospital anyway.

When we arrived at the hospital the doctor told us Edwin had died before they brought him in. A nurse took us in to see him and for a final good-bye. I thought to myself, *"That can't be our son."* He looked very much like he was just sleeping. We asked the question, *"Why us, Lord?"* Now years later we can see the Lord's will in it all, but at the time we were in shock and couldn't think right. A nurse took us to another room. There we met the state troopers who asked us questions of how it happened. That was really hard. We were deep in grief and could hardly answer.

Neighbor Mary Dawson took us back to Sams. I would rather have gone somewhere and just be alone for a while, but people were there and it seemed there was no place to go.

We called Ammon's parents and told them first. Next

we called my two unmarried brothers who were at home. Many phone calls came in from Pennsylvania. We were thankful for the people that were praying for us, and felt so blest by that.

We decided not to start for home until after dinner on Sunday. Sunday morning a minister from a church at Shiloh came to hold services for us. We arrived safely home at 9:00 p.m. Sunday evening.

We could hardly believe all the kind friends and neighbors that came that evening, and the days following.

I would like to encourage people to talk about it when they experience something like this. That is one step in the healing process.

We didn't have any other children at the time, but one year later, on October 29, 1974, we had another son whom we named Clyde. Then came two daughters, Diane in March 1976, and Ileen in June of 1980. When Ileen was seven weeks old my mother, Reba (58), was killed in a head-on accident while driving for the Amish. She died in the van that we had taken to Ohio when Edwin died.

Memories

A trip to Ohio the family did plan,
We all wanted to go in a rented van
To visit Lillian, Mabel and Sam —
Not knowing the will of God's plan.

We traveled at night, so the hour would not be late,
We left Harold Martin's at quarter after eight
On Friday, October 12, 1973 at night
So that we would arrive by Saturday daylight.

We traveled for miles and miles and more miles
Till all were tired and sleepy and no smiles,
We stopped by the road to take a rest
So all would be feeling our best.

At seven-thirty Saturday morning we arrived at Sam's —
The family from Pennsylvania in a tan van.
We were so happy to see each other again —
The first time Lillian saw Doris Ann.

But four hours later God called Edwin home
From this world of sin to no longer roam.
Our hearts are filled with sorrow
But You give us hope for a bright tomorrow.

We, as a family, God, often ask "Why?"
But You will make it plain by and by.
We know Your will is the best way
So we look to you for comfort day after day.

May we all be ready to meet on Heaven's shore
So we will all be together forever more.
We thank you for Jesus who died for our sins,
Arose from the grave victor o'er death's sting —
He made it possible to spend eternity with Him.

—Mrs. Harold (Mildred) Martin

—Ammon & Floretta (Flossie) Burkholder
Shiloh, Ohio

Louise Brubacher

August 19, 1986 to July 21, 1997 (10 years)

A Birthday Never To Be Forgotten

Irene Brubacher, Mother

A misty, wet morning it was. We decided to only do the main laundry and leave the Sunday clothes for another day. After the hired girl, Naomi, had the washing started, I headed for the pea patch.

While picking peas I reminisced over the activities that took place Sunday and the reunion we held here on Saturday. The birds entertained me while cheerfully voicing their individual songs into a melody. I had a peaceful setting and the pail was soon filled with peas. With eagerness Louise, our oldest daughter, brought an empty pail to me. She was ready to start shelling peas. She knew she would earn money while shelling. But I didn't realize what all lay behind her grin.

She had been over by Mommy (Grandmother) to bake

a Double Fudge Chocolate Cake for my birthday which would be the next day. Then after dinner she went over to ice and decorate it. As she had shared the secret with Dad, she told him she thought the cake would be cold enough to put the icing on by afternoon. When I was once more out in the pea patch, cards were being made.

We give our children two cents per cup for the peas they shell. They did really well, but they didn't give me a chance to sit down with them. And so the morning went. I often did not have my pail filled until one of the girls came for more. Most often it was Louise who came, always with a big "we beat-you-again" smile. Mid-morning our son, Mark, and his cousin, Wayne, also came and helped pod peas. After dinner Naomi helped pick too, so then we made faster progress.

While we were picking, Ruth and Louise started singing. By now it was warm and hazy, and the music sort of just drifted down to us, yet very clearly. *"Twilight is stealing over the sea, shadows are falling dark on the lea."* Over and over, they sang it. It made a queer stir in my heart. I remarked to Naomi, "There's something about their singing — they can sing together quite well by now." There was just *something* in the very air, but I couldn't put my finger on it as to what it was.

After Naomi and I finished the picking, we both walked up to the house. The boys had gone fishing. Naomi started podding peas and it really tempted me to sit down and join them also. It was such a happy circle beneath the old apple tree. Doddy (Grandfather) was also helping. But no, I'd better start blanching the peas.

Soon everyone was in the house with Louise's eyes sparkling while saying she gets thirty-two cents this time. That was the most she ever got at one time. This time

I said, "Well, I'd better give it right away." After taking care of her money she disappeared over to Mommy's to piece together another puzzle. Her aim was to put in one hundred pieces at one length of time, and she often got many in.

Our daughters, Sharon and Ruth, then wanted to help fill milk boxes with peas. Oh! There come the boys with their fish. After putting the kettle of water over to boil for macaroni, I took the last of the peas to the freezer with a feeling of satisfaction. I thought we had a worthwhile day. (When the macaroni got cooked, I don't know, because — our lives were to be changed soon.)

Waah! Mark brought in his crying little brother, Frank. Apparently Frank thought he should help clean fish too, cutting deeply into his thumb. I was bandaging him up and changing him when an out-of-puff Doddy opened the front door saying I should phone for the ambulance. "I drove over Louise." A short, stunned silence followed. "Well," I wondered, "how is she?" "She just lies there." "I'd better phone then."

By the time the final directions were given, my voice was shaking. Naomi held crying Frank while I ran out the door — the very same door Louise had so cheerfully gone through only minutes before. It seemed she would hardly have had time to don her boots and milk cap. Out she had gone to help bring in a calf from the pasture in the farthest corner. And she had the privilege of driving the loader tractor because the boys were busy right then. So Doddy and Louise went, but now he came in alone...

Grabbing a bike, I pedaled back our scenic bush lane, not seeing even one tree, only wondering when I'll see the tractor. Down one hill and up the next I went, on and on. Finally, there it was halfway down an incline where Doddy had braked to stop. And there was Louise trying to sit up, waiting, watching, and asking the boys for me, her mother, to come. After climbing over the fence Mark and Wayne backed away a bit. They had gone out straightway when Doddy came in, so Louise wasn't alone long. But oh, the anguish — to see her in such pain! I quickly told her to lay down — down on the wet, muddy lane where the cows meandered back and forth on their path. The baby calf was nowhere in sight and the cow was back a piece watching on.

I could plainly see where the back wheel went over Louise, straight across her chest, below the arm pits was one muddy streak. Her apron was torn off and lying back a piece with her milk cap. Louise painfully said, "Oh, I hurt all over."

Fighting back tears, and in want of saying something, I asked, "Where do you hurt?"

She repeated, "Oh, so badly all over." All the while I could hear a rushing rumble going around in her abdomen. And she was frothing at the mouth with her tongue pointedly going back and forth. Speechless prayers ascended. The thought that Louise might be leaving us was most evident. But while she could yet talk, I just couldn't give up *all* hope. And to say good-bye — well, I just could not. I told her I phoned for help and that an ambulance would come soon. It would have been easier to just cry with my arms around her, but Motherly love couldn't do much to ease the pain. I stroked her forehead all the while. I knew I should be saying something, so instead of good-bye I told her, "Jesus can help you so you don't hurt so much," but there was no response. Again I said, "Jesus can help you so you won't hurt so much." She nodded her head and was soon semi-conscious. Then the first fireman (a near neighbor) had arrived.

Once the fire trucks and crew came they applied oxygen and tried to get her heart beating, but could only hold it for three or four seconds. She would open her eyes whenever they called her name. Now I know how little response that really was. At the time I thought it didn't look too good.

Wishing that Lester was home, my mind and heart seemed to have retreated. Mechanically, I tried to think what needed to be done next. After answering questions for the police, the ambulance was soon there. By then I thought I'd have to hurry and get ready to go with the ambulance.

Still having some hope for Louise, I was visualizing a long stay in the hospital. I threw various things into a bag and put shoes on my bare feet. Then I tried to tell Mommy how serious it was, but she seemingly had her mind on our little four-year-old Nancy who was crying hysterically. Frank was wide-eyed in Naomi's arms. The other two, Ruth and Sharon, were full of questions. For once I didn't pay much attention. I didn't want the ambulance to wait on me.

It all takes time. The accident happened around 5:10 p.m. and left again at 6:15. Near the barn hill were some deep bumps where Lester had dug with a backhoe and hadn't graveled it again. (The backhoe was still on the tractor making extra weight when it went over Louise.) As the ambulance bounced across those bumps, I wished I could have borne those bumps for her. But once we were off and away with a police escort, there was no time wasted.

Lester was on his way home, and nearly there, when he saw the ambulance going over the hill and away. He came through all the many vehicles and cameras. Someone quickly directed him behind the barn where another policeman questioned him about different things on the tractor. Then he was driven to the hospital.

I recognized several neighbors near our lane as we went. There were quite a few red traffic lights and at each one a policeman had stopped the traffic for the ambulance. In sixteen minutes we were at the hospital — less than half the time it usually takes. I heard Louise once on the way, but God had sent an angel for her before we reached the hospital. The doctor at the hospital worked on her for twenty minutes. Had I known, I would have told them to stop.

I was led to the room where Louise lay. But I wasn't prepared for the utter quietness that prevailed the whole room — and, oh, the peace on her face — our oldest daughter, nearly eleven and almost grown-up, in size... I had often pled on my knees for wisdom and patience to guide her strong nature in the right way. She was a willing helper when her backache let her work, always putting zest into whatever she did. And now, here she lay — so utterly at rest. Finally, a nurse said, "Oh don't be so brave about it," and gave me her shoulder to cry on. I looked at Louise a little more, then went back to my room and phoned home saying, "It's all over." What more could I say?

My sister, Ruth, had come home soon after we had left. She didn't know at all what the big commotion was, neither was it pleasant to bike through a crowd of cameras. But at least Naomi wasn't so alone with the children then. Ruth answered the phone and received my short message, then spread the word. So sudden and shocking it was! People were the least suspecting when answering her call.

Lester and I went to see Louise once more, alone. After quietly talking and looking, I said I have such a longing to comb her once more, seeing her hair was so muddy and untidy. A nurse who knew we don't keep snapshots, snipped a tuft of hair and put it in a tube saying, "Here is a remembrance of her long braids."

We left the hospital with the thought in mind that our children needed us at home. We came home to a kitchen full of neighbors and relatives. Plans were made for the funeral. (The morning's clean laundry waited patiently in baskets.) By and by the visitors left. After answering the children's questions as good we could, we put them to bed, and we finally went to bed too. We wondered how Doddy's felt. Could they sleep? We went to bed, but not to sleep. Our thoughts traveled fast, one chasing the next. We were hardly able to believe that it really was so, yet we wanted to be submissive to our Father's will. Lester was wishing he would have been home at the time of the accident as he couldn't picture the scene or Louise's pain as I described it. And oh, there were many things I wished I could have done yet for Louise. I had feelings of guilt for failing so often as a parent.

Psalm 51 caught my eye while I was paging through my Bible the next morning, *"Have mercy on me, O God, according to thy loving kindness: according unto the multitude of thy tender mercies blot out my transgressions... The sacrifices of God are a broken and a contrite heart, O God, thou wilt not despise."*

Lester found comfort in Revelations 7:17, *"For the Lamb which is in the midst of the throne shall feed them, and shall lead them unto living fountains of waters; and God shall wipe away all tears from their eyes."*

The new morning brought many willing hands. The house and barn, once more were made ready for the next occasion, but hardly like the Brubacher reunion we had so eagerly prepared for only a few days before. The children could hardly wait until Louise's body was brought to the house. They had wanted to go with me when I went with my mother and Lester to comb her. At last, the day came when Louise was in our house once again. Frank was eagerly making "aye, aye" on her. Mark and Ruth quietly looked on, while Sharon and Nancy were full of questions. "Why do you cry if she is happy with Jesus?" To the younger ones Louise was as a little mother, and to Mark she was nearly an equal playmate. The two of them did many things together. Now Louise was gone, leaving Mark alone with only memories of those happy times.

Louise's short mission in this life is over, but may we who are left behind be true to our Savior. She surely must be enjoying bliss undreamed of by man. Our loss is her gain. Now she can hold our baby Wayne. In Wayne's short stay here on earth, Louise would often say, "Meha missah ihn so oft haeva vieh meah kenna." Translated from Pennsylvania Dutch: "We must hold him so often while we can." Wayne was born an anencephalic baby in 1990, and lived only five days.

One boy, who hadn't been able to come to the reunion because of a broken leg, came on crutches for the viewing. His birthday was the same day as Louise's, but not the same year. Many were the school children that viewed Louise's face once more — a face that was without its usual smile. She looked so at rest, as though she could have only been asleep. Louise's teachers and classmates came for a last farewell. They knew her as one who enjoyed meeting people and learning to know them while trying to be a friend to them all.

The day after Louise's death was my birthday — a birthday never to be forgotten. Naomi knew where Louise's card was as she had helped design a scroll on the card. The children gave me Louise's card along with their own. Her card was black with white lettering and roses. The verse was so fitting for the occasion.

Selebrate your birthday
in your very favorite way,
With your friends and family to share
your extra special day.

We looked at the birthday cake Louise had baked and decorated just for me, then we froze it, not knowing when we would eat it. People suggested that we eat it on Louise's birthday. That is what we did — twenty-nine days after her death. It was our last chance to sample her baked goods, so it was eaten with mixed feelings.

A poem Louise often recited while doing the supper dishes comes to my mind. She would say it most plainly and with much expression. Her game: "Playing Ball" is finished in this life.

Play Ball

This world's a diamond with bases laid,
And on it life's great game is played.
The teams are human beings versus fate,
TIME is the umpire watching at the plate.
We're at the bat, our purpose o'er and o'er
To wield ambition's bat and try to score,
And lam that sphere where not a fielder goes!
Some of us seem to bat with skill immense,
Knocking long homers o'er the deep field fence;
Others bunt infield hits, but wildly race
And beat the ball down to the primal base.
Still others, though they strive their best, no doubt,
Fan wildly in the air, and then... strike out.
They seek the bench downcast, with visage drawn,
Crestfallen, shamefaced, blue - - ambition gone.

Oh rag the umpire, growling like a bear.
"You robber! That decision wasn't fair!"
That's not the game; be not a grouch or a quitter,
What though you're not a .500 hitter.
You've got another chance, stand at the plate -
Grab tight the bat, get braced, and calmly wait.
Wait for a good one, let the others rip,
And when it comes along - - NOW - - lam it hard
and ZIP!
It's got to go and so must you, young man,
Hike for the base - keep going - - yes, you can!
Steal second . . . go . . . easy . . . not too gay,
There get a lead, A HIT - - now you're away!
Keep on, don't stop, don't lose that dandy stride,
You've got to beat that throw-in - - - SLIDE NOW, SLIDE!
HURRAY! You did it! Score? Of course you scored!
See - - there's the tally marked upon the board.
And now you'll win the game, no doubt at all,
You just can't lose, young man,
IF YOU'LL PLAY BALL.

—*Poet Unknown*

With the hope we have in Jesus Christ we know Louise got Home to her reward.

—*Lester & Irene Brubacher*
Elmira, Ontario, Canada

In Memory of Louise Brubacher
Daughter of Lester & Irene Brubacher
Died July 21, Almost Eleven Years Old

The sun was lowering in the west;
there rose a gentle breeze.
It's time to start the evening chores;
where is our fair Louise?

They saw her going back the lane
to bring the cows on home;
But little did she realize this
path no more she'd roam.

One cow, she seemed to lag behind,
she did not want to yield;
No wonder for a newborn calf
lay alone back in the field.

How soon this motherly instinct
shows in maidens young and bright;
For who would leave a little calf
alone out there all night?

So Doddy and lass with the loader
went to bring this calf to barn;
The lane was rough,
they slowly drove when suddenly there was alarm.

There in between the tractor wheels
there rose a piercing cry;
Was this the way God had it planned,
a cruel way to die?

As mortal man does older grow,
reflexes they get slower;
Ere this machine was in control
another wheel passed over.

What grief and anguish Doddy felt
as he did hurry home;
In haste the mother hurried back
where her child in pain did moan.

Life's evening sun was sinking fast;
although some words were spoken,
Before she reached the doctor's place,
all earthly ties were broken.

She did not see a future life
with sin and sorrow blighted;
She did not see this joyous time
when cow and calf united.

She did not see her mother's smile —
with glee she had surmised,
For Grandma helped her bake a cake
Mother's birthday to surprise.

What she now sees is beyond all words,
where joy and peace are given;
Thousands of children are gathered there —
such is the Kingdom of Heaven.

So Father, Mother, children dear,
in time now cease your weeping;
Some day you hope to see her there,
oh, what a joyful meeting!

—Noah W. Bearinger

Eldwin Martin

September 23, 1974 to September 2, 1997 (22 years)

Amy Martin

January 16, 1976 to September 2, 1997 (21 years)

Conlan Martin

June 25, 1997 to September 2, 1997 (2 months)

Special Rainbows — God's Promises

Shirley Martin, Mother & Grandmother

In 1984 our family was asked by the church to leave our families in Maryland and move to poor Clay County, Kentucky to help with the church work there. Of course there were many adjustments to make as we changed from a farming and dairying occupation to a butchering and produce farming occupation.

Through the years God had blessed us as a family. In

January of 1996 our family consisted of five boys and two girls: Eldwin (21), Wendell (19), Matthew (16), Elbert (13), Brenda (10), Ethan (6), and Kendra (3).

It was a special year for us. Eldwin and Amy were married in January and started a produce and greenhouse business of their own, twenty minutes away.

Wendell and Brenda were married in December of the same year and lived next door to help with the home business. Our small business had grown, and we needed their help. Life was special with two daughters-in-law joining our family. We spent many happy times together.

The year 1997 was a year to be remembered. The first cloud and shadow was standing by Wendell and Brenda as she lost her mother to liver cancer only three months after they were married.

It was a busy summer ahead with all of us involved in our produce work. Right during the busy cabbage harvest little Conlan Jay was born to Eldwin and Amy on June 25. How happy we all were with a little baby to hold and love — our first grandchild!

A few weeks later, Eldwin called one evening and said, "Mom, are you seeing the beautiful rainbow? It is so pretty against the dark sky!"

I answered, "No, it is pouring rain here." (The photo he took of that rainbow was so special later!)

The summer produce was coming to an end. We did not grow late produce since we reopened our butcher shop in September each year. Eldwin and Amy, with some other families, were still busy as ever growing late peppers and selling them wholesale. They often combined the loads that were going to Cincinnati, Ohio, three hours away.

September 1, we reopened the butcher shop. We were not aware that Eldwins were getting a big load of vegetables ready to leave in the early morning hours. It was so late when they got their load together that they decided to drive the load to Cincinnati and sleep there until the warehouse opened.

On Tuesday morning, September 2, we had just risen from a good night's rest and were beginning our day together in prayer as husband and wife when one of the boys knocked on our bedroom door. They informed us that Lauren Rudolph, our deacon, was at the door wanting to talk to us. We were completely unprepared for the shocking news he had to tell us. Eldwin, Amy, and baby Conlan were on the way to Ohio with a load of produce and were all killed at one o'clock that morning in an accident.

Of course, questions surged through our minds. What happened? Where? Why?

The accident had happened an hour from home. The coroner from that county had called their home county funeral director. He then passed the message on to one of the church families that he knew. They, along with our deacon and his wife, brought us the sad news. They also took care of informing others about the accident.

First we called Wendells and told them to both come to the house. The rest of the children were awakened too. My brother and his family lived close to Eldwins and worked with them a lot in their produce business also needed to be told.

Amy had been raised by her grandparents who lived close by us. (Her mother had deserted her as a two-year-old.) Her Grandpa's first words were, "God took all our roses." They had been so happy to see Amy married as a Christian girl, because the rest of their family were out in the world. When Conlan joined the family, he was so special to them.

As daylight appeared that morning, we sat together as a

family with my brother's family. Our church families came to be with us and to do what they could.

We were told that a tractor-trailer driver was stopped along the interstate, partly on the road yet, to pick up a woman. He was just starting out again. Authorities told us that Eldwin's Isuzu box truck slid a long ways and crashed into the back of the tractor-trailer. The whole cab was pushed back into the box of the truck, killing all three instantly. The woman along the interstate had fled the accident and it appeared as though the driver had tried to pull away from the scene, by the show of oil puddles on the road. Some other truck drivers had seen the improper actions of the truck driver a few minutes earlier and were talking about it among themselves on their C.B.'s. When the 911 call went in, they understood what had happened. These drivers were used as witnesses later, although they didn't see the accident happen.

Eldwin's body wasn't released right away, because it was sent for an autopsy since he was the driver.

In making the funeral arrangements we were told that we wouldn't be able to have a viewing. Oh, so final! How could we grasp it all?

On Wednesday, we found out where the truck was towed after calling those who were investigating the accident, so our family, Wendells, and my father decided to go see the truck. My mother wondered why we wanted to see it. I said, "We need to see the truck to face reality."

That ride past mile-marker seventy-five wasn't easy... We saw vegetables scattered along the road, black skid marks, and oil leaks. We took pictures of the skid marks from the van window.

When we arrived to where the truck was, the officer was at first reluctant to let us see the truck. Finally he said,

"How many want to see it?" Daniel answered, "We all do." So he led us through a garage to a fenced-in area.

How heart-rending! Eldwin's hat was lying on the truck floor. The baby's car seat was smashed. It was easy to see why they were killed instantly.

The funeral was planned for Friday. In the meantime neighbors and community people brought food or just stopped by. The accident made quite an impact on the community. The Laurel County newspaper reporter titled the accident report with the words "God Had Something Better." (Quoting from a sister in the church who was interviewed about the accident.) Many folks from the community came to meet us at the Paces Creek Mennonite Church on Thursday evening. Family and friends from Maryland had arrived too.

On Friday morning, as we gathered for the funeral, we saw more friends who had traveled to share this time with us. It brought tears to our eyes to think that so many had come just for us. What a comfort brethren and sisters in the Lord are at a time like that!

Eldwin and Amy loved to sing. They often sang together as they worked. As the chorister at church, the last song Eldwin led was *"My Jesus, As Thou Wilt"*.

When we first entered into their house after their deaths we were drawn to the song on their refrigerator. This song is sung to the tune of *"Where Could I Go?"* which you will find in the *Christian Hymnal.*

Where Shall I Go?

Lord, here I stand before Your Holy Throne,
Facing a future all unknown;
Young and untried - yet trusting You to guide-
Show me the way You'd have me go.

Life lies before me beckoning me on,
My heart is filled with youthful zest;
Channel my zeal, Your purpose to fulfill;
Just use me Lord as You see best.

Well, I may face some disappointment keen,
Hopes shattered round my feet may lie;
Sorrow and care my lot some day may share,
Still may I say "Lord, here am I".

Though it may seem my life is all in vain,
Though men my labors may not see;
All is worthwhile, if I may see Your smile,
Gladly your servant I will be.

Chorus:
Where shall I go? And what shall I do?
Seeking a purpose for my life;
Longing to serve, Your kingdom to preserve,
Help me to say, "Lord, here am I".

Brother Arvin read this song at the funeral saying, "They answered God's call with *'Here am I'* early Tuesday morning."

The next weeks many cards arrived in our mailbox from far and near. We sat around the table together each evening to open our mail. One evening a local businessman, who often stopped to visit us, stopped by as we were opening our mail. He sat down and looked at each piece of mail with us.

During the next weeks, many thoughts went through our minds. Did Eldwin fall asleep? That was hard to accept, because we knew there would be more trips with produce.

A lot of that meant early morning hours on the road.

One day I said, “If only we had the baby.” But Daniel said, “Remember, we would still be grandparents, not parents.” There was no lonely, grieving partner. They all went together.

Another painful job was to take care of their earthly possessions. Since they had not been married very long and did not have much, we decided to sell their things at a “church and family” sale. While going through their things, we found photos of the special rainbow Eldwin had called us about.

A few weeks after the accident, we received a scrapbook from friends and family. A month later we were given a second book. The ones who fixed those pages had no idea that we would soon face another shadow.

Wendell and Brenda made plans to move onto his brother’s farm in January. They spent the next few months helping us through our busy butchering season.

We were looking forward to the birth of our second grandchild. Late on the first day of November, Wendell called to say baby Janice had arrived. We woke our sleeping children to tell them the special news. The girls wondered if we could stop at the hospital to see her the next morning on the way to church. We said, “Maybe.”

At eleven o’clock that evening, Wendell called again to say they needed to airlift Janice to a bigger hospital. Daniel and I left for the hospital, which was only five minutes away. It was too foggy to fly Janice as planned so the ICU team came by ambulance for her.

What was ahead? We couldn’t sleep when we returned home early that Sunday morning. It was still too early to call anyone, so we sat down with the scrapbook. The first poem we read, “Tomorrow”, was what we needed.

In His hands I leave tomorrow,
For my heavenly Father knows
What is needed for my future;
When it comes He will disclose...

Sunday morning Brenda was released so we took Wendell and her to the hospital where Janice had been taken. Little Janice looked so pitiful hooked up to so many wires and tubes. She had started having seizures too. What was her problem?

That Sunday afternoon as we left the hospital, God sent another special rainbow across the sky. His promises are sure — He will never leave nor forsake us.

After spending ten days in the hospital, Janice was diagnosed with Zellweger's Syndrome. She was sent home with oxygen and a feeding tube. She had no muscle tone and didn't move. It seemed she didn't see or hear. She had her ups and downs in the next seven months, but she was always "Little Janice" and grew very little. The little girls at church liked to hold her. We all loved little Janice, but she never responded with a smile.

On May 25, 1998, Janice's little body wore out and she joined our family in heaven. Brenda said, "I lost my mother, my best friend, and my baby." It was a lot to experience the first year of marriage. Again we all felt the prayers of family and friends.

Almost a year after the accident we were drawn into a law suit by Amy's father. We were required to appear in court. He was trying to get money from the trucking company. It was so painful to have to relive it again and again. Through it all, we did find out from an actual witness how the accident happened. The truck driver did not have his emergency signals on. Eldwin could not have seen that the truck was not moving at night. He never even braked. Those skid marks weren't his. They had been on the road before. Daniel had asked the officers how he could have skidded so far and still hit so hard. They could never come up with an answer.

Does time heal sorrow? Yes and no. When we were planning Matthew and Wilma's wedding, three years later, it seemed it would be best to plan it between the closing of the produce stand and the opening of the butcher shop. Also, we had to consider when it would suit Wilma's family. We decided on the first Saturday of September. We suddenly realized it would be on September second. Could we have a wedding on that day? That seemed to suit best, so we went ahead with those plans. So, that day has been a bittersweet one for us.

Two weeks after Eldwins' accident, we went to Pennsylvania for the annual Conservative Mennonite Teacher's Institute. The theme song was "Suffer the Children to Come to Me." That song still brings tears to our eyes, as does the last song Eldwin led at church.

We, as Job, have learned to say, *"The Lord hath given and the Lord hath taken away; blessed be the name of the Lord."*

We have received much from God's hands. Wendell and Brenda now have two healthy boys, although they were told Zelweger's Syndrome is a genetic problem and could happen again. Matthews also have a healthy little girl. We also have the blessing of the young family who left their family in Maryland to live in the house Wendells left and became our helpers until Matthew got married and moved into that house. They helped fill the void in our family as brother and sister, and their children are like grandchildren to us. They live close by.

At the time of this writing our family's graves are the only ones at our church. The church was built in 1993. Before that we only had a rented building and no grave site. In 1990, our youngest son, Ethan was born weighing only one pound and ten ounces. He spent two and one-half months at the hospital. We thought he would be our first family loss, but God had other plans. He is now a healthy boy, and we needed to give up his oldest brother first. God's ways are always best. Someday we'll understand.

Our daughter Brenda, who was young, loved to write poetry. She put her feelings in words, which were our feelings too. The following poem is one of the many she wrote.

Remembering the Story

A strong healthy couple, a dear little son,
Their smiles and their singing would cheer anyone!
Together they lived with their goal in full sight,
They worked for the City where cometh no night.

These folks had a farm with so much to be done;
They labored from dawn till the setting sun;
Each person that knew them could surely declare,
They were such a pleasant, industrious pair.

Memorable evening for those who were there
September the first - there was joy in the air,
That last Monday eve when they worked on a load
Of vegetables, then they would head for the road.

They started out early without a despair,
So little they knew of the danger out there;
But soon they were heading on I-Seventy-five.
An accident left not a one still alive.

That day was much weeping for those left on earth;
The Word says life's ending is better than birth-
So let us accept it as God's holy plan,
He's provided glory for each righteous man.

The funeral came and much people did share,
The burden the families were called to bear;
They helped ease the sorrow - we thank everyone,
The days without Eldwins on earth have begun.

Our minds often take us way back to the days,
When Eldwin's while working would sing songs of praise;
When they were still dating - we watched them come out -
We had to be quiet, we were not to shout!

Their wedding day dawned with much joy in the air,
How sacred the happenings going on there;
At Eldwin's home many a cousin and friend,
Were watching as into a home two did blend.

Twas soon - 'bout a year and a half after this,
That Eldwin and Amy rejoiced in much bliss-
A dear little boy whom they named Conlan Jay,
Had come to their home on that bright joyful day.

These memories help us to mend in our heart,
For 'tis very painful from loved ones to part;
But thankfully we have those times long gone by,
Those happenings precious become when folks die.

So e'en if we laid those dear ones in the grave,
E'en though one more look at their face we would crave,
We have to remember they'll have no more pain,
Up yonder in Heaven's wide beautiful plain!

—Brenda L. Martin, Sister
1997

—Daniel & Shirley Martin
Manchester, Kentucky

Janice Loreen Martin

November 1, 1997 to May 25, 1998 (6 months)

A Special Gift From Heaven

Brenda Martin, Mother

The sun had already set on November 1, 1997 and many of our family were retiring for the night. For us, our cup of joy was running over. Our firstborn had arrived, a little girl. We named her Janice Loreen. However, our joy was short-lived. We detected the nurse was trying to get her to breathe and the doctor seemed a bit puzzled. Without us seeing or holding her, they took her from our room to the nursery. After about an hour they let us walk over to see her. Something didn't seem right. Our baby was lying so still and her facial features were not like most babies'.

They called in a respiratory doctor. He inserted a tube through her navel for oxygen. He came into our room and told us the only problem was, since Janice was born early, her lungs weren't fully developed. She only weighed five pounds and eight ounces. He told us they would need to transfer her to another hospital to give her treatments to help develop her lungs. She was transported by ambulance at 1:30 a.m.

When they discharged me from the hospital, Wendell's parents took us to see Janice. Seeing her hooked up to monitors, a feeding tube, and oxygen was hard. If only we could be home, rocking our little one and feeding her normally. This certainly had not been part of our dream. They let me hold her for the first time. I also fed her through the feeding tube.

That night we stayed at the Ronald McDonald House. During the night Janice had a light seizure. They started her on Phenobarbital.

The next day a genetics doctor came in to see her. He thought she looked like she had Zellweger Syndrome, but needed to do a test to be sure. The test returned positive. Janice had very little muscle tone, and could only suck a little at a time out of a bottle. The feeding tube was placed through her nose where it stayed for the rest of her life.

We were almost sure she could not see or hear. She also needed oxygen often. After we told the hospital staff we didn't want her hooked up to a respirator or anything besides oxygen, they started planning for us to take her home. Since there were no other children at home that needed us, we spent most of our time with her. We knew the basics of caring for her. They often let us feed her, change her feeding tube, change her diaper, and bathe her. We just needed to learn CPR before we could take her home. We brought Janice home on November 12 at the age of eleven days.

We found her care quite a challenge once we were home and away from the nurses. We missed having no one there to tell us whether we were doing everything right. Janice had her ups and downs. Some days we could get her to drink her whole feeding from the bottle. Other days we could try an hour and hardly get anywhere. For a while she only got two ounces at a feeding. We were hoping to have her graduate from the feeding tube, but she was just too weak to get that accomplished.

When Janice was almost two months old, we took her to Maryland for Christmas vacation, and to celebrate our first anniversary. (We were married in Maryland.) Janice did well, so we went again in January for my father's wedding. My Mother had passed away in March 1997 with liver cancer.

In February we were to the doctor for a checkup. They were very concerned about Janice. She had been without oxygen for a month. Her color was not good so they put her back on oxygen and she responded well. She had a cold soon after that and her bottle feedings didn't go good at all.

About a month later Janice had what we thought was another seizure, so the doctor increased her medication. Around the middle of May she started with a fever. Sometimes Tylenol and Motrin could hardly keep it down. Janice had an infection, but the doctor couldn't discover where it was. She also had internal bleeding. Zellweger babies can have a Coagulation Deficiency, and this was the first we noticed it in Janice.

Things seemed to clear up for about a week. Then two days later, May 23, the bleeding began again. We took Janice to the doctor and they gave her an antibiotic shot. That night her gauze was soaked with blood where she had got her shot, and the bleeding hadn't stopped yet. It was still bleeding the next day.

During the night her fever had gone up to 104.6 degrees. Janice's heart rate was dropping and her lungs sounded congested. The doctors didn't encourage us to hospitalize her because of her condition. It was a hard decision — to think of doing nothing for her. Nevertheless, we knew eternal rest was awaiting our weary one.

On May 25, soon after the dawn of a new day, the angels came to carry her from her mother's arms — safe to the arms of Jesus.

In some ways it was quite a relief for us, and yet, our arms were now empty. Then there was the thought of needing to go through the funeral and laying her to rest beneath the cold sod. We were thankful for all the family and friends who traveled from Maryland and Pennsylvania to share our evening of grief. The viewing and funeral were Tuesday evening at Paces Creek Mennonite Church.

Time does have a way of healing these deep wounds. Our loved ones always hold a special place in our hearts. When we remember that the Lord works out all things for His glory, we can rest in the fact that He knows best.

It is healing to talk of your experience and share with others who know the pain. It's also very special when those who have never lost a loved one are willing to listen or remind us that they still remember our loved ones.

God has blessed us richly in the past four years. Two energetic boys are now our daily joy and responsibility. Our desire is to be united in heaven where there is no sorrow to dim our joy.

—Wendell & Brenda Martin
London, Kentucky

Arvin Laray Eby

August 30, 1983 to November 4, 1999 (16 years)

Doris Eby, Mother

November 18, 1948 to March 26, 1997 (48 years)

"Plucked By The Angels..."

Fonda (Eby) Hege, Sister

The following account was written by Fonda with some information and wording taken from her brothers' and sisters' writings.

It was going to be a special day! The men had put in many long hours in getting the site ready to set the house trailer. Our brother Carl, Rosanna and family were moving a used house trailer in and starting a business on a corner of the home farm, and today was the day to set the trailer.

It was cool, cloudy, and breezy, but that didn't dampen our good spirits. The tan trailer was hitched to the tractor, with Daddy driving, as it slowly moved down the driveway. We spotted sixteen-year-old Arvin, the youngest of eight in our family, inside the trailer adjusting a window. He gave us one of his jolly grins and a good hearty wave — he was as excited as the rest of us!

Slowly, slowly the trailer bumped its way across the corn stubble in the field. They stopped once to check inside to make sure everything was traveling well. As they neared the site Daddy slowly swung the tractor and trailer around so he could drive onto the foundation as straight as possible. The men were all around, motioning and guiding, while attempting to get everything aligned perfectly. All together it was brothers Carl and Arvin, brothers-in-law Robert Diller and Duane Strite, four-year-old Jeffry Strite, and Rosanna's brother Levi. We laughed at Jeffry who was trying to do man's work, copying their example. When everything was lined up, they chucked the front tractor wheels to prevent it from drifting down hill.

Next they hooked up the generator to warm the house trailer so the women and girls could begin painting. Then the men began their job of removing the wheels and axles from under the trailer. Of course, they needed to jack the trailer a little higher to do so. They kept blocking it up as they went. After they removed the wheels, they began to let the trailer back down onto piers with the jacks, block by block. Daddy and Robert worked under one beam while Arvin and Duane worked under the other. Robert began to get suspicious their pier was tilting a bit, but wasn't sure. Then he heard Duane ask Arvin, "What was that noise?" Arvin replied, "Oh, it was just the blocks shifting." It was getting really windy so Robert decided to quickly crawl out to see if the wind was swaying the trailer. On his way out he heard a creaking and crunching. Frantically he reached back to grab Daddy, but was too late. The trailer crashed to the ground, tearing Robert's coveralls.

We women and girls were inside the trailer at the time, casually discussing dresses. The impact nearly threw us off our feet. We heard someone holler and one cried, "Someone is pinned underneath." Thinking it was Robert because he had hollered, we ran to the back door, and what greeted us but a deathly silence. There, still, too still, was our beloved Daddy, doubled underneath the trailer. Robert ran for the truck and rushed to the farm for the loader tractor. Carl ran for the skid-loader but it wouldn't start, so instead he and Rosanna sped to the farm to call 911, and to tell Mom (Step-Mother). She also contacted our sisters, Darlis was at work, and Karen was at her home. This was not real — it could not be true. We bent over Daddy and called, "Daddy, Daddy!" but there was no answer. I cried to sister Diane, "We already lost Mother, must we lose Daddy too?" Mother's death, just a little over two-and-one-half years before was still fresh in our memories. She had passed away from liver cancer at the age of forty-eight years.

Suddenly Diane thought of her husband, and ran to the other side to find him. Duane's legs were pinned under the trailer, but eventually he was able to work himself out. He told Diane, "It's too quiet under there," referring to Arvin.

Rosanna's sister, Lena, and I were still with Daddy when suddenly I thought about Arvin. I hoped for all the world he was in one of the trucks that had gone to the farm. But no, here came Levi saying that Arvin was underneath the house trailer and there was a steel beam across his chest. Levi began using a handyman jack to try to free Daddy, but it kept slipping. Robert arrived with the tractor, but Levi motioned to him not to try lifting the trailer, but to come help him free Daddy. They tore off the skirting that was around the bottom of the trailer to get to him better. Seeing how blue he was, Robert decided he must get him out, although it was dangerous to move a person with probable back injuries. Gently they slid him, rolling him out of his doubled over position. The blue left his face, but he was so ashen. Carl and Robert gave him artificial respiration and then heard a gurgle. Robert needed to keep his fingers in Daddy's mouth to keep his airway open. He also prayed to calm them both, not knowing if Daddy could hear.

Medical equipment and neighbors began pouring in the lane. I didn't want to see any more as I was afraid of seeing Arvin. I went to the farm where I called sister Brenda in Kentucky and brother Kevin, who was teaching school. I told Kevin to come right away, but since Brenda was miles away I begged her, "Just pray." While I was gone they put Daddy in the ambulance with a neck collar on.

John Horst, an excavator, was on his way home nearby when he was contacted to come with heavier equipment to help lift the trailer. So he quickly came with his big loader. Merle Petre, a neighbor, began digging a ditch with a shovel where Arvin was so they could pull him out.

John Horst's loader, and two other loader tractors, worked together at lifting the end of the trailer. The men blocked it up as they lifted. Uncle Clifford Eby and Merle Petre reached in and pulled Arvin out by the shoulders of his coveralls. They slid him onto a poly-board stretcher. Someone suggested oxygen but the chief said, "Keep right on moving. Keep right on moving." They loaded him into the waiting ambulance and left right away. Carl and Rosanna followed the ambulance to the hospital.

When I got back to the accident site I found out that a helicopter had been called for Daddy. The dreaded thought hit me, "If Arvin is the worst why are they taking Daddy in the helicopter instead?" We knew the answer deep in — Arvin was gone, and they knew it! Yet we clung to hope... Maybe, maybe he would be all right.

Soon we saw the helicopter coming from the west mountain. It circled and landed a good distance away in the field. Daddy, under a maze of wires, sensors, brackets and restraints, was transferred from the ambulance to the helicopter. It looked so pitiful to see him in such a helpless condition, with Daddy totally unaware of what was happening. Before long the helicopter lifted and flew to the hospital.

Duane was also under medical care. They put a splint on his injured leg from his hip to his heel. They also hooked him up to oxygen and I-V, although they reassured him he probably didn't need it. He too, was soon on the way to the hospital. Diane was allowed to ride along in the front of the ambulance. Uncle Leonard Eby (Daddy's twin brother) and wife, took Mom, sister Darlis and I to the hospital where our injured family members were.

The minutes seemed like hours. Our hearts were full of unanswered questions. Darlis even asked, "Will life ever be happy again?"

Meanwhile, Carls arrived at the hospital and reported that they were there to be with Arvin. It wasn't long until a social worker came and told them she needed a contact person to identify Lester Eby (Daddy). Carl thought Daddy had been flown to Baltimore, Maryland, so he figured they had Daddy and Arvin's names mixed up. But lo, when he got there it was Daddy! There was a swarm of trauma unit personnel around him. They asked Carl a few questions and sent him back out. Not long after, they called him back to identify Arvin. Soon the rest of the brothers and sisters were arriving at the hospital. The social worker came along out with Carl and directed us all to the trauma unit doctor's personal office. The doctor was to be with us shortly to give a report on our loved ones. When she arrived the look on her face warned us that the news was not good. She told us they did everything they could for Arvin... then came the sentence that changed our lives forever. "Unfortunately Arvin had 'unsurvivable' injuries." Carl wanted to make sure everyone understood her statement, so he told us that Arvin was gone. We all cried together... Could it be true? Our dear youngest brother, so lovable and loving, and full of vigor and youth was gone. The doctor went on the explain Daddy's case. His vitals were all good. He was not yet conscious and his brain seemed disturbed. Since he had received a blow to his head she wanted to send him for an MRI and x-rays. She also said he was losing the ability to move his right leg. We hoped and prayed for his recovery.

Our bishop and his wife came in to be with us. Since the crowd was getting large, a social worker took us to a large waiting room. We all felt so empty, exhausted, and sad. Yet we were so thankful that God spared Robert and Duane, who so narrowly escaped. After all, minutes before the trailer fell, all seven of the men were underneath.

Duane and Diane were kept informed with what all was going on. Duane was given pain killer for his leg, which made him sleepy. Later, when he went for x-rays, Diane came to be with the rest of the family.

We sat together, waiting and waiting for time to pass. The social worker came and told us we would be allowed to go see Arvin's body if we wanted to. So we took turns going in small groups. As we went through a maze of corridors, Carl stopped us and warned us what Arvin would look like so we wouldn't be surprised. "Because of the impact on his chest, blood vessels burst under the skin all over his face which made him look blue. This was due to asphyxia. His chest was full because he had been on a respirator. We arrived at his room and stepped around the curtain. There lay dear Arvin's body, yes, just the body. The real Arvin was Home with his Maker. How thankful we were that he was a Christian. It eased our deep grief to know that Arvin was ready to go.

Our weary minds and broken hearts tried to grasp the fact that Arvin would no longer be with us. Wasn't it a dream? But he laid so still, and his injuries proved the stark reality that it was real. But his hair still looked so normal. Darlis and I stroked it lovingly. It was the same ruffled, dark brown hair, although his handsome face was blue and swollen.

When we were back in the waiting room someone brought us a little plastic bag of treasures they had found in Arvin's pockets. It was his pocket knife, his watch, and his treasured Leatherman All-Purpose tool that Floyd, Darlis' boy friend, had given him for his sixteenth birthday only two months before his death.

We also got word from Daddy again. His x-rays showed his back was broken below the waist. He also had some broken ribs, but his vitals were all good. Only time would tell whether he was paralyzed or not. What anxious moments?!

The doctors decided to move Daddy to ICU from the trauma unit. So the social worker took us up to the ICU waiting room. We were so glad for this helpful social worker. She took such good care of us and our needs.

When Duanes got reports back from his x-rays, they were overjoyed to find out that there were no broken bones, only a torn muscle that would take several weeks to heal on its own. After he was discharged, they came to be with us. Duane came on a wheel chair.

Around 3:00 p.m., Mom and sister Karen went back to see Daddy. The nurse encouraged Mom to talk to him although he would probably not respond. He was on a respirator and heavily sedated. When Mom talked to him his eyes moved under his eyelids. The nurse exclaimed, "He heard you!" He even squeezed her hand when she asked him to.

Later, they let him come out from under his sedative a little to see if he could move his legs. Praise God, he could move both of them! He was so restless and the nurse had to work to keep him still so that he wouldn't further injure his back.

Around 4:30 p.m. Mom, Darlis and I went home to get better clothes on. While we were gone Diane and Karen went to see Daddy. The nurse welcomed them saying, "He has a surprise for you!" They walked into his room and he was off the respirator. Another step forward! He only had an oxygen mask on. They greeted him with, "Hi, Daddy!" He opened his eyes and his first words were that dreaded question, "What happened?" They told him that he was in an accident and got hurt. Then he asked, "Was anyone else seriously hurt?" The girls wanted Mom to tell him, and so the nurse told him he needed to rest. They felt so cruel walking out without answering him. Daddy told them later that he fell back to sleep as soon as they left the room and couldn't even remember they were in, or that he had talked to them.

When Mom and we girls arrived back at the hospital, Mom and Carl went to talk to Daddy. Again he wondered what had happened, so Carl and Mom told him that the trailer shifted and fell. They told him about his own condition. Then he asked if anyone else was hurt. So Mom told him about Duane's legs getting hurt. That satisfied him for a while, but then he asked if anyone else was hurt. So they told him about Arvin's injuries. Finally, he asked, "He's not gone, is he?" No longer could they evade the truth so they told him that Arvin went to be with Jesus. A very pained expression came across his face. The truth hurt so much. We all felt so badly for him, needing to bear such grief in his weakened condition.

Mom and the six of us children who lived locally gathered in Dad's room early that evening. We took turns talking to him and holding his hand. We wept together as Daddy brokenly said, "But Arvin, Arvin! I can hardly believe it!" He told us he is not blaming God. We told him not to blame himself either. He told the girls he was so glad their husbands were not killed. Mom stayed with Daddy almost all the time after that. The nurses were so kind to them both. The nurse promised us she would care for him like she would if he was her own dad.

Family and friends poured in that evening to be with the family. Many kind hands helped with chores at home on the farm and at Roberts and Duanes.

Sister Brenda and her husband arrived safely from Kentucky around 10:00 p.m. We were glad they had a safe trip.

The family all returned to the hospital in the morning. The day was filled with visitors. We also made funeral arrangements, planning the funeral for Tuesday in hopes of Daddy being able to be present. The doctors said they couldn't promise, but there was a possibility that he would be able to go by Tuesday.

The surgeon decided the swelling in Daddy's back was going down enough that they would be able to surgically repair the break that night. He left for surgery around 6:20

p.m. and we began the long wait. We were told that they would call partway through to let us know how things were going. They had allowed one-half hour prep time and three to four hours in surgery. But when three hours were up and we had heard nothing, we began to get very anxious! One of the family suggested prayer. So Uncle Leonard Eby led in prayer pleading for God's presence and that thing were well with Daddy. Thank God for the power of prayer. It helped to calm us. Sure enough, fifteen minutes later at 10:00 p.m., they called out to the waiting room and said that things were going well, but they needed another hour and a half to finish.

The next few days were painful ones for Daddy as they coached him to take a few steps. He kept progressing well, although he was very weak.

Monday afternoon and evening was Arvin's viewing. Daddy was not able to be there, so someone stayed with him over that time. Hundreds of people came to the viewing, and oh, what encouragement they brought to us.

Tuesday dawned sunny and warm, but the clouds of sadness were hanging low. We were thankful Daddy's condition was stabilized enough to come to the funeral, although nearly every move or bump in the road hurt him. He arrived at Clear Spring Church in an ambulance just before the service started. They wheeled him into the back of the church house on a stretcher. Our family gathered around our brother's casket one last time. The tears were flowing as we viewed his precious body. This was the only time Daddy got to see Arvin after his death.

Then a nurse wheeled Daddy's stretcher up the center aisle and the family followed. We found our places at the front of the church. It was a full house with an estimated 750 people present. Two of the ministers that had part in the service had also been Arvin's school teachers. The sermon was titled, "Till He come." It was a touching service, and yet encouraging to hear how Arvin's short life had richly touched others. It also gave us hope to watch, and be ready when He comes.

We sang three songs throughout the service: "Thy Will Be Done," "Life On Earth Is But A Vapor," and "The Last Farewell."

Six boys (Arvin's friends) carried his casket out to the grave. After the grave side service, we watched as the ground was filled over the grave. Dear Arvin — forever gone from our view — but always in our hearts. His final resting spot was next to our dear mother's. We are grateful to God that we could have had the privilege of spending at least sixteen years with Arvin, for it is better to have loved and lost than never to have loved at all.

The days that followed were not easy ones as we tried to find a new normal. But we were kept busy with our own work besides running back and forth to the hospital to see Daddy. God was good and Daddy progressed well. He wore a body brace whenever he was not lying down. Eleven days after the accident he was discharged from the hospital. We gladly waited on him, "hand and foot". He kept diligently trying to do more and more for himself. Around three months later he happily laid aside his brace. He is thankful to live free of pain, although he does find that his back tires more easily. He also had to retire from the rigorous exercise and demands of farming.

—Lester & (Doris Eby, deceased): Mary Eby
Clear Spring, Maryland

Minerva Eberly

November 5, 1960 to February 22, 1979 (18 years)

Kathy Eberly

November 3, 1957 to February 22, 1979 (21 years)

Sonya Eberly

April 6, 1974 to February 22, 1979 (4 years)

Life Must Go On — There Will Be A Way

Henry & Hilda Eberly

Parents & Parents-in-law & Grandparents

Thursday, February 22, 1979, our daughter, Minerva went to work at Martin's Farm Market. She worked in the bakery where her other sisters had worked. She would go in at 4:00 in the morning and make donuts to fill their many orders, and for the store. After finishing the donuts, she helped ice cakes, cookies, and buns.

It was a cold, but sunny day. Henry and I went to our friends who had a small butcher shop to butcher a beef and a hog.

In the evening, we, and our six youngest children went to our daughter, Mabel and Roy Sensenig's home at Nottingham (one-and-one-half hours away) to see our new grandchild. It was their first child. She was born on February 19, 1979 and they named her Janelle Kay. We were almost home again when a carload of boys stopped us and told us Minerva was in a serious accident.

There were people at our house when we got home. We already felt the many prayers ascending to the throne of grace. We were told to got to Ephrata Community Hospital because Minerva, Kathy, Sonya, and some friends were involved in an accident. We took our son Henry along because he needed to identify Kathy and Sonya.

That night was a sleepless one.

"For whether we live, we live unto the Lord; and whether we die, we die unto the Lord: whether we live therefore, or die, we are the Lord's" (Romans 14:8).

Minerva was the fifth child of our eleven children. She was a very ambitious, healthy girl and loved to be where the action was. She was baptized at the Weaverland Conference Fairview Mennonite Church along with twenty-one other young people in 1977. Minerva was in the bloom of life when she was called home in the twinkling of an eye at 8:30 p.m. on February 22, 1979.

The car she was a passenger in skidded on an icy stretch of road and collided broadside with a tractor trailer truck on Route 322 between Hinkletown and Ephrata. There were six people in the car and they all died instantly. The truck driver was a member of our church. He stood by compassionately until everything was taken care of, which we are very thankful for.

There were approximately 1500 people at the viewing at our home. The funeral was held at the Fairview Mennonite Church and the burial was in the cemetery there.

We received much support spiritually and many offered material deeds of kindness.

"And we know that all things work together for good to them that love God, to them who are the called according to his purpose" (Romans 8:28).

—Henry & Hilda Eberly
Richland, Pennsylvania

Aaron Weaver

August 19, 1975 to November 28, 1996 (21 years)

Thanksgiving Tragedy
Edna Weaver, Mother

It would have been helpful to have a book like this to read when we needed it most in the sudden passing of our son Aaron on Thanksgiving Day, 1996. Stories of children's sudden death help me to better understand my feelings and actions over the time of Aaron's death, feelings that I didn't understand at the time.

Aaron was number seven in our family, the youngest son, but had five younger sisters. He was a healthy baby. I felt we should give him a strong, solid name. He did have a swollen left leg, but had no problems with that. Much later we found out he has congenital lymphadema, which means he had no glands to let the fluid out of his leg, causing it to swell. When he was about eleven, he was hospitalized with infection in that leg. After that he always needed to wear a special elastic stocking which needed to be replaced every two months. After two months the stocking was stretched too much, which caused infection, and he needed to stay off his feet.

At age eight Aaron fell hitting his head on a stone causing him to get grand mal seizures. These always put him to bed for two days. He was put on the third different medication till he had the right one, so had many unpleasant days.

Aaron was always cheerful and had lots of friends. He did everything on his part to make friends if he knew someone didn't like him. He was always singing or whistling. One of his favorite songs was, "Heaven Will Surely Be Worth It All". He did not want people to know about his health problems. He also had slight asthma problems from babyhood on. I often wondered how he could live a normal life if he would ever get married, which I knew was his desire when he was older. Noah and I often prayed for him.

Aaron and Alvin, the brother next older, were such close companions so it was hard on Aaron when Alvin moved back to Wisconsin where we used to live. Alvin lived alone in a small house. We asked Aaron to stay here in Missouri, at least till he was twenty-one, and he promised to do that. In August, on his twenty-first birthday, he left for Wisconsin to pursue a waiting job.

It was so hard to see him go. The tears just came. I didn't know why because the older ones had left too. Aaron knew it was hard on me. He gave me a hug saying, "I can always telephone." After he went out the door, I cried uncontrollably. I often shed tears for him after he left. Unknown to me this was the last time we would see him alive. In three months he was gone.

The week before Thanksgiving he called telling me his stockings were worn out and he still hadn't taken time to find a supplier. He always needed to be measured for a special order, which was hard. I scolded a little knowing he would soon be down with infection. He informed me I needn't worry because he won't live long enough to need them. I was puzzled, but don't know why I didn't question him. Upon telling the rest here at home, I found out he talked like that to some of the others, too.

On Thanksgiving we went to church. A few of the girls went to a wedding. The rest of the day we spent at home. I had invited a bunch of company for that next Sunday and was planning what all needs to be done in the next couple of days.

After we had gone to bed, we got a phone call from our son-in-law in Wisconsin. He told us Aaron was in an accident on the way to a youth singing, but knew no details. Later Alvin called from the singing, but didn't know either how bad it was. He did think Aaron was being taken to the hospital. We called our girls to come home, and also called our married son in Pennsylvania. We tried again and again to call to Wisconsin, but just couldn't get through. Quite a while later we got a call with details of the accident, and the shocking news — Aaron had been on a bike and was hit from behind by a "hit and run" driver, who was later found and had been drunk. Aaron was instantly killed from a broken neck.

Sleep did not come that night for any of us. We did a lot of praying. This was our first close contact with death. My dad had just passed away in October due to cancer, that was 1,000 miles away. The next day was cold and dreary. We felt so very much alone till close to noon when friends and relatives came to help make funeral arrangements. Noah took it really hard — kept blaming himself.

In Wisconsin they had funeral services then the body

was shipped to Missouri where we had funeral services, and where Aaron was buried.

It just didn't seem real before the body was here. We anxiously waited for Aaron to come home. The undertaker had fixed him up so we could view him. He had that mischievous grin on his face. It seemed he was only sleeping peacefully like I often saw him sleep after he came home from chicken-catching at night.

His death did not seem real till we followed the hearse out the lane, then we knew he would never return. The tears just flowed till they put him in the grave. When they shoveled dirt down on the casket — such a forsaken, helpless feeling. His youngest sister took it so hard. At this time, and long afterwards, the girls went through a hard time. They were afraid to go out at night by themselves, and even afraid to go to bed.

In the long days and weeks that followed we waited breathlessly for mail and visitors. Beings the weather was mostly cold and unpleasant, we had very few visitors. Every day we quickly did our chores, hoping someone would drop in to visit.

We got close to eight hundred cards and letters. They meant so much. We read them over and over. We still go back to read them even though it is over two years. Over this time we often didn't understand our feelings and actions. We were easily hurt by things we heard other people say. I know now people were just talking like I too often did, not thinking how others might feel. Aaron's brother, Alvin, was having a hard time accepting this death. For weeks he didn't go into their little house knowing he would be reminded of Aaron everywhere. Instead, he slept on the floor in his sister's house, which was close by.

Whenever I missed Aaron so very much, I prayed and

thanked God for taking him in his youth. For a long time I didn't sleep well because of too much thinking, trying to figure out where we could have done different to avoid this happening.

One night Aaron came to me in a dream. He didn't say anything, but traveled with us a distance in a van. He seemed so happy and kept smiling. After a while he just drifted away, and it seemed no one else had seen him. In my dream I went home feeling so light and happy. I was singing and working again. After this things went better for me.

After going through Aaron's things, we found his Bible. He had plainly marked where to read for different kinds of problems. I'm thinking maybe he had more trouble accepting his infirmities than we realized, although he never let on to us.

On Aaron's first birthday after his death I was feeling so sad. I didn't understand why. Then the children in other states all called, and we even got some cards that day. They must have known how I'd be feeling.

Quite a few people gave either flowers, or money for flowers, in remembrance of Aaron. So now we have a flower bed which we call Aaron's flower bed. Aaron loved flowers like his dad does.

—Noah & Edna Weaver
Versailles, Missouri

Harvey B. Nolt

May 18, 1982 to May 2, 1991 (8 years)

Grandfather's Namesake

Ella B. Nolt, Sister

"Hurry up, Harvey," I called impatiently. Younger brothers could be so slow! I was eleven and he was almost nine. Since it was the second to last day of school, I was in a hurry to get home. Harvey's hat had blown off and he had to climb off his bike and run after it. Now he was ready to get on, but why did it take him so long?

I was slowly biking on and the three neighbor children were even farther ahead. I cannot recall exactly how it happened, but I looked back as Harvey went flying through the air into the field. A car had hit him! I threw down my bike and ran for him. He laid curled up on the ground, with blood lying in a pool around his head. Was he still alive? I laid my hand on his chest and was relieved to feel his heart still beating.

The driver of the car stopped and came over. I suddenly felt afraid. Would he do something to Harvey? He turned the boy over roughly, put his head on Harvey's chest, and cried, "Oh, no!" Apparently Harvey's breathing had stopped.

More people stopped and were gathering around. I decided to go home and tell Mom. At the top of the hill, I met Mom coming. The neighbors had already notified her. Dad was plowing in the back field, and I went to tell him. It was the hardest thing I ever told him — that Harvey had been hit. As we walked up from the field together, he asked a few questions to get an idea of what had happened.

Mom went to the hospital with the ambulance and an acquaintance took Dad in. Then my youngest sister, Adeline, and I were left alone. Oh, what a lonely feeling! The neighbor came over and said we shall go to their place for the time being.

If they take Harvey to the hospital, he will be all right, I thought. Nevertheless, I could not concentrate on the chatter of the little girls. It seemed so out of place. About 5:00 p.m. Mom called. "You can come home now," she said in a strained voice. "Harvey died."

That evening neighbors and ministers gathered at our house to discuss funeral plans. It all seemed like a dream, as did the days to come. (There was no more school that spring because of Harvey's death.) Neighbor women came to help clean the house. Feeling listless, I went outside and sat on the swing. It was the first time I didn't feel like doing anything at all while in perfect physical health. I thought of writing in my diary, but someone must have stuck it away. It was nowhere to be found.

The undertaker brought Harvey's body a few days later. I didn't want to, but we all gathered around and watched while he opened the coffin. It was the only time I ever saw Dad cry.

All my Nolt cousins from Pennsylvania came. We had fun, but not like usual. It didn't seem right to be laughing and playing while my brother lay silent and still in the living room. Many had been our squabbles while he was still alive. Oh, why hadn't I been a better sister?

Why do people hesitate to talk to family members about the deceased person? Sure, it may hurt to talk about it, but it is a healing hurt. If the hurt just stays inside it is harmful. I think it is especially important to get children to talk about it. Some will talk about it without much prompting, but others will not. With time, healing will come.

Our Only Son

Luke Nolt, Father

On April 28, 1975, my father Harvey H. Nolt died of injuries from a bike/car accident. Seven years later on May 18, 1982, God gave us a little boy whom we named after his grandfather Harvey. This was the only boy in our family. We had two girls. Ella was older than Harvey and Adeline was younger.

The happenings of May 2, 1991, are still very clear in my mind. It was springtime and we were in the midst of planting corn. I was hoping to finish planting all that was plowed. I went to the field with the planter and Harvey brought the fertilizer wagon, then walked home to go to school. I did not realize this would be the last time I would see him in this life.

Mid-afternoon I started plowing an old sod field so when Harvey comes home from school he can take over the plowing. After a few rounds I saw Ella come running over the field. When we met she said, "Harvey had an accident."

"What does he do?" I asked.

"Nothing," she answered.

My first thoughts were — maybe a few bumps. We went to the house. A friend who was at the accident scene on the way home from work saw us and stopped. He offered to take me to the hospital. I still didn't think it could be serious, but he said, "It's bad."

On the way to the hospital we stopped at the scene of the accident. The only people there anymore were the unlicenced, intoxicated driver of the car, the State Highway Patrol, and a neighbor who had been working in his field and saw Harvey fly through the air after he was hit.

The accident that took the life of my father and the one that took the life of our son were almost identical. They happened at the same time of year, both victims were riding bike and were hit from the rear with the front right side of the car scooping them up, and the head hitting the lower right corner of the windshield, putting a dent in the windshield and causing severe head injury. Otherwise, there were no broken bones or damage to other parts of the body.

When we came to the hospital reality hit me as I realized death was at hand. Harvey still had a faint heartbeat and they were making preparations to send him to a larger hospital by helicopter. We didn't want that at all, but finally okayed it under the condition that they remove life support if he would be like a vegetable. The helicopter was delayed because of high winds so they gave us the choice of having life support removed or not.

A few minutes later the doctor came and said, "Life is gone." He paused. "You made a wise decision. If this were my son, I would have done the same thing."

I still respect that doctor.

We were able to see Harvey before we started for home. He looked so natural, but this was only a perishable body, for "dust thou art, to dust returneth." Knowing that funeral plans, and life, must go on and having a tape measure in my pocket, I measured him for a casket — almost five feet and only eight years old. With heavy hearts we went home. It was hard to call family members to let them know...

The next morning, not knowing what to do, I went out early to finish planting corn. It was almost easier to cry out in the field with God close by. Soon a neighbor came and took over planting. Neighbors and friends came to help get ready for the funeral.

The body was brought here Saturday and viewing was on Sunday. Monday morning, short services were held at our home, then came the time for the funeral procession to the church. I almost had to cry when coming to the church with the yard full of people — to think they all left their homes, families, and work to show their respect to us, was a very unworthy feeling.

There was a final viewing, then burial with short services and the song, "This World Is Not My Home," at the grave site. The main service was held in the church house, including the song, "Safe In The Arms Of Jesus." Harvey had picked this song in school the day before his death.

The text was from I Peter 1:24. It still brings tears to my eyes when this scripture is quoted in church. Both his grandfathers were mentioned in the funeral sermons. One was nearing death because of a brain tumor, the other had died in the same manner as Harvey. The death of his aunt

Ida Brubaker was also mentioned. She died October 15, 1966 while visiting friends in Canada, at the age of nineteen years, when a drunk hit the buggy she was riding in.

At the time of Harvey's death the dogwood trees were in full bloom. This brings pleasant memories every year.

Questions did arise — why us, with only one son? At the funeral service it was said that God, too, gave His only son. Where would our hope be if God had not done this? What a great and merciful God we have.

We would have liked to care for our son longer, but we know he is being cared for much better than we could have done. We want to be like Job was when things were taken away from him, that we can say, *"The Lord has given, the Lord has taken. Blessed be the name of the Lord."* And like David said when his child died, *"The child cannot come to me, but I can go to the child."*

The night is coming. Let us labor in the Lord so we can go to be with those loved ones who have gone on before.

Withered Flowers

Nora Nolt, Mother

About 3:15 on Thursday afternoon I got a phone call from my neighbor lady telling me Harvey was hit by a car. *"Probably he has a bloody nose or something like that,"* I thought. "Should I come down?" I asked.

Hearing how shaky her voice was when she replied, I suddenly started thinking it could be serious. As soon as I got to Harvey lying on his back in the field, I thought he was gone. The only injury to be seen was a little bleeding from his ear, but he was blue from not breathing. His heart was still beating. Later, we were told that in a healthy body the heart can continue beating about twenty minutes after the breathing had stopped. It seemed so long till the ambulance got there. A lady who was passing by was doing artificial respiration till they came.

In the emergency waiting room a nurse sat beside me trying to strike up a conversation. I felt sorry for her because I was not one bit interested in anything she asked or said. She soon gave up and just sat there.

On the way home from the hospital I said to Luke, "Now Harvey won't have perfect attendance after all." The next day was to have been the last day of school. But it was then decided to end the term without going another day. The scholars said, "Who feels like having a picnic?"

Our families all live in Pennsylvania and Wisconsin, so our neighbors gathered in our home to help make funeral arrangements. One would have thought the community's schedule was already full, but time was found for a funeral. Saturday was to be preparatory services; Sunday, communion; Monday afternoon, examination meeting; Tuesday, bishop ordination; and Thursday, Ascension Day service. So the funeral was planned for Monday forenoon.

Several days before Harvey's accident he brought some dogwood flowers into the house. Luke had helped him pick them and told him the legend of the dogwood being used for Jesus' cross and the flowers representing the nails and the blood stains. We put the flowers in a jar of water. Later, I took them out of the jar, probably to make room for more sweet potato plants.

The morning after Harvey's death I found these flowers, now wilted, and thought *"...just like Harvey's life."* The Bible says, *"For all flesh is as grass, and the glory of man as the flower of grass. The grass withereth, and the flower thereof falleth away."* So I Peter 1:24 was chosen for the funeral text.

My seventy-year-old father was ill with a brain tumor. On Friday one of my brothers called to say Dad was very low. We wondered if there were going to be two deaths in the family at the same time but four hundred miles apart? But Dad's condition improved enough that my brothers all came for Harvey's funeral. Kind friends stayed with Mom and Dad till my brothers were home again. Dad died seven weeks later.

Harvey's viewing was Sunday afternoon and evening. Our brothers and sisters, and some aunts and uncles were here for supper. I was so glad my sister-in-law planned the meal because even thinking of food was a chore. I absent-mindedly filled my plate like usual, then thought, *"I can't eat all this!"*

My sister's oldest son was two years younger than Harvey so I had been sending Harvey's clothing to her as he grew out of them. My sister and her husband were leaving for their home in Wisconsin on Tuesday after the ordination. I thought that's a good opportunity to send Harvey's clothes along, so I packed them. It really wasn't hard, perhaps I was still in shock, and handling his clothes was just an everyday thing. But then several days later it was different when I found his barn coat in the closet as I was doing the laundry.

Adeline, age six, often spoke of how she misses Harvey. She said, "He was my friend." A poem someone sent us expresses it so well.

The Child's First Grief

Oh, call my brother back to me,
I cannot play alone
The summer comes with flowers and bees -
Where is my brother gone?

The butterfly is glancing bright
Across the sunbeam track;
I care not now to chase its flight -
Oh, call my brother back.

The flowers run wild - the flowers we sowed
Around our garden tree;
Our vine is drooping with its load -
Oh, call him back to me!

He would not hear my voice, fair child!
He may not come to thee;
The face that once like springtime smiled,
On earth no more you'll see.

A rose brief, bright life of joy,
Such unto him was given;
Go - thou must play alone, my boy!
Thy brother is in Heaven.

And has he left his birds and flowers?
And must I call in vain?
And through the long, long summer hours
Will he not come again?

And by the brook and in the glade
Are all our wanderings o'er?
Oh, while my brother with me played,
Would I have loved him more.

—*Selected*

My heart went out to Harvey's school friends.

In the following days when something interesting was going on we thought we would like to share this with Harvey. But we knew these earthly things are nothing compared to the glory the Lord took Harvey home to. It's like my brother-in-law said, "Harvey isn't missing a thing."

Something we treasure is a sentence Harvey wrote for a spelling lesson on April 16, 1991. It reads, *"Did you ever imagine how nice it is in heaven?"*

We are so thankful God let us have Harvey for almost nine years.

—*Luke & Nora Nolt*
Plymouth, Ohio

LAMAR F. MARTIN

April 10, 1981 to June 19, 2001 (20 years)

Called To Beulah Land

Edna Martin, Mother

In the year two thousand one
The nineteenth day of June,
Dawned a perfect summer day
With roses all a'bloom.

The Master Gardener unknown to us
Selecting from the bowers,
Chose the choicest, dearest one
Lamar, from midst of ours.

Life was young and full of promise,
The future seemed so clear
And little did we realize
Death's angel hovering near.

Waters snuffed the breath of life,
All earthly help was vain.
He'd crossed the Jordan's foaming tide,
Our loss is His great gain.

He's gone, his chair is empty,
His smile we'll no more see,
His voice is but an echo
Etched in our memory.

We now turn to the promises
That Jesus gave His own,
His children will be reunited
When we reach that Heavenly Home.

—M. H.

How blessed we felt that spring when our second son, Lamar, was born. Unlike his dark-haired brother, this boy had light brown hair and blue eyes. He was only a few days old when our family doctor noticed that his eyes looked blurred. He sent us to a specialist who told us Lamar has congenital (present at birth) glaucoma. The specialist sent us to an Eye Institute where Lamar had his first surgery at two weeks of age. At thirteen weeks he had his fourth and final surgery, which left him legally blind in his left eye. At least the eye pressure was now under control. The last years of his life, he used several different drops to control the pressure, which had risen again. Lamar never complained much about using the drops.

As a school boy, Lamar was very shy. He was always very nervous about reciting poetry at the Christmas program. Yet, as he got older the shyness left him and he made friends very easily. About eleven months before his death he started dating a young lady by the name of Sharon Huber. She was a member of the Weaverland Conference Church, the same as Lamar was. We appreciated his choice. They seemed so happy together!

The last Sunday evening they were together, it seemed it was so hard for him to leave. Did he sense that it would be his last date? Lamar's two cousins, Joshua and Wilson, and his friend Marvin joined him as they went to the cabins for a few days. Lamar's uncle and boss, family, and friends were already there. They had an interesting time Monday and part of Tuesday. One time they went to a little country store where Lamar bought a candle for Sharon. Tuesday forenoon, Lamar and the other boys planned to go to a clearing called Beulah Land. Lamar asked his uncle Jere if they want to go to Beulah Land too. His uncle said, "No, just tell us how it was when you come back."

In the afternoon Lamar truly left for Beulah Land — never to come back again. After dinner the boys decided to go for one last swim before starting for home. They were having a good time swimming when Lamar called for help. We will never on this earth know exactly what the cause was that he needed help, but we must accept it that God wanted him at that time. He was only a short distance away from safety — a rock. His friends tried their best to help him, but to no avail. He was only under the water five to eight minutes, but we feel life had already fled when they pulled him to the bank.

We were picking cherries at a neighboring farmette when we received the news. Only those with experience know what it is like to receive such shocking news. They told us it didn't look good at all. We then left for home, and were just coming up our sidewalk here at home when the call came that he was beyond medical help. Lamar was at home with God.

It is now fourteen months since Lamar has left us. We still miss him, his cheerful ways, and happy smiles. One great consolation we have is a vision one of his best friends (who was along at the time of Lamar's drowning) had several nights after Lamar's drowning. Lamar was walking toward the gates of heaven with a look of wonderment in his eyes. In this vision a small child was sitting beside the path. Lamar picked the child up, and took it along toward the gates of heaven. How like Lamar, as he dearly loved little children and was loved by them! We loved him, but God must have loved and wanted him even more!

Gone But Not Forgotten

Life was enjoyed to the fullest by a dear young lad
A friendship blossomed with Sharon which
made the heart glad
Many dreams were shared, with Christ
the most important one
As Lamar left Sharon's place, a key chain
his attention won
Remember "you're special" were his parting words
that night

Friends went camping, enjoying fellowship
and nature's beautiful sight.

Merrily the boys were enjoying the cool water until
"Oh no!"
A boy was struggling, Joshua wanted to rescue
but had to let go

Realizing that the Lord sent angels to carry Lamar home
To the golden gate where saints need no more to roam
Indeed our dreams are broken, but we must try our best
Nestling close to God until He calls us to Heaven to rest.

—Ivan & Edna Martin
Fleetwood, Pennsylvania

Mervin Shertzer
December 13, 1982 to April 30, 1987 (4 years)

Melvin Shertzer
February 23, 1988 to October 29, 1997 (9 years)

Sharon Shertzer
January 25, 1991 to August 20, 2000 (9 years)

Carolyn Shertzer
October 5, 1981 to October 22, 2000 (19 years)

Ties That Bind
Ruth Shertzer, Mother

November 25, 1978, was Ben and my special wedding day! The theme verse for this special occasion was from Psalm 127:1. *"Except the Lord build the house they labor in vain that build it."* One song we sang was, *"O Father Lead Us... thro' ways of darkness, where we cannot see - fears oft affright us, doubtings walk before, O heavenly Father lead us now, and evermore!"* My thoughts were touched, and I blinked back tears to wonder, *"What does God have for us to face in our unknown future pathway of life?"* God has a purpose for every new Christian home for his glory.

After a short, happy wedding trip, we lived in the town of Millersville, Pennsylvania. Ben worked with his father on a dairy farm about two miles away.

As time went on God granted us dear, healthy, precious children. With thankful hearts, we felt so blessed.

When Eunice was 5 years old, Carolyn (4), Mervin (3), and Nathan (1) we would take the children along with us to the farm. But as time went on we felt the need to move onto a farm where we could raise our children.

Mervin, at three years old, was a duplicate of his daddy. I can still see him in my mind, having the Lancaster farming newspaper laid out on the kitchen floor as if he was looking for a farm.

After much prayer and seeking, the Lord opened the door to a place in Juniata County, Pennsylvania.

We were so thankful to be living together on a family farm by March of 1986. Mervin enjoyed every cite of farming. He wanted to grow up to be Daddy's helper! The four children played church on the barn steps with their dollies. We planted potatoes to sell, and raised turkeys to butcher for Thanksgiving and Christmas. Eunice, Carolyn, and Mervin helped dress these turkeys while Nathan watched. It was a special family time. Grandpa Shertzers came to help a few times too.

In the winter of 1987 life changed. We noticed that Mervin (4) seemed to hold his left knee straight when going the stairs. I asked him if his leg hurts. He answered, "No!" I was concerned, but then he went out to play in the snow. After playing, he came in the back door of the house, almost crying for help. I hurried to carry him in. He said, "I can't walk right! My leg hurts!"

When Ben came in he called the doctor, asking for an x-ray on his leg. But our family doctor was on vacation, so they advised us to go to the Camp Hill Hospital. The doctors seemed concerned and wanted to admit him. We weren't ready for such fast decisions! Ben asked if we couldn't go to a closer hospital, so they let us go to Hershey Hospital. There they admitted Mervin for three days. They took tests and x-rays of his leg and lungs. The doctors wanted to take an MRI too. This was very scarey for dear little four-year-old Marvin. They laid him on a bed that slid into a dark tunnel. Thankfully, the nurses let us stay with him. Ben reached into the tunnel and touched his head while I touched his feet. Then he was more relaxed.

We were constantly praying, asking God to have mercy upon our dear son, hoping health would be granted to him.

Ben went home after the tests. We anxiously looked forward to seeing each other the next day, but my strength failed. To be left alone with this responsibility...

They put Mervin in the monitor room where two other children were. So I wasn't able to sleep in the room with him. I waited till he slept, then I was supposed to sleep in the playroom on a cot. During the night Mervin awoke and saw I wasn't with him! He got out of bed and looked down the hall for me. A nurse came and he quickly hid behind a curtain at the door so she doesn't notice him. The nurse told me how she found him and put him back to bed.

Morning came and I went to see my dear anxious boy.

He said, "Mommy, where were you? I couldn't find you." I felt so touched. I thought my heart would break — to feel the nearness, and love, and the support we needed from each other.

Unknown to us, this new day was going to be a very stressful one. The tests had revealed that Mervin's knee cap was deteriorated and there was a tumor inside his bone marrow. The doctors wanted to take a biopsy of the tumor.

Before Ben arrived at the hospital in the morning, the nurses took Mervin and I down to a room where we waited for someone to come get him. Mervin was so nervous, and I felt so alone without my husband at my side! I tried to comfort my dear boy, but it was more than I could do by myself. Mervin begged that we come to him as soon as they are done with his leg. *"Poor boy, they probably won't let us in the recovery room."*

A nurse came and laid Mervin on a stretcher and quickly wheeled him down the hall. I wanted to walk along with him to ease his fear. But the nurse said, "Say good-bye to Mommy," and away they went. He tried to look back at me, and cried, "Mommy, Mommy, Mommy!" Then they disappeared around a bend in the hallway but I could still hear Mervin crying for his Mommy!

I stood there alone — with no one around, I cried for my fearful little boy. Then someone walked by and asked if I'm all right. I tried to be brave, yet I was hurting inside. I was wondering what my little boy must face before they put him to sleep for the biopsy.

Someone helped me find my way back upstairs. I was so glad to see Ben when I entered the waiting room.

After what seemed like a long time, we heard a child screaming and crying as the elevator moved from floor to floor. We wondered whether it might be Mervin crying. We quickly went to the elevator and the door opened. What a terrible feeling! Little Mervin was crying fearfully. He had lots of pain and was throwing himself around on the bed. There was a cast on his leg. That puzzled us. What a good feeling it was to be with our son again, but how we pitied him — the awful pain he had to go through. The nurse finally gave him a pain shot.

The doctors then came and talked to us at Mervin's bedside. They said they had to cut into the bone two inches to get the tissue samples out. The cast was necessary to save his leg from breakage since the bone was weak.

In a few days we took Mervin home. Oh, how we wished that this would be his only hospital experience and he would be on the way to recovery. But it wasn't that easy. After a few days we were again on the way to the hospital for an appointment. Mervin had been enjoying himself at home...

Daddy carried his precious son, with cast on, into the hospital. We went into a small doctors' room. Dear Mervin looked so scared, and our hearts pounded heavily. "This is not going to be an easy hospital stay." The doctor explained to us what they found on the MRI test. "We found an Asteogenic Sarcoma (cancerous tumor) in the bone marrow." What is he going to say next? "...amputate left leg, take part of lung away, and give strong chemotherapy."

Ben asked, "How much chance do you give Mervin if all this is done?"

The doctor said, "Twenty-five per-cent, but we want to give him a chance!"

Ben braved himself and asked, "How long would you say he would live if you wouldn't do anything?"

"Around four months," replied the doctor.

Our thoughts were battered — such a blow! Surely God will intervene for us. All we need to do was trust His great power for our dear son. Surely he will not need to suffer all these experiences.

The doctor then left the room, and Mervin told us, "I'd rather go to see Jesus than to go through all that!"

We were surprised to hear our four-year-old was so resigned to life. How sweetly we smiled at him and said, "Yes, Jesus loves you."

We took Mervin home. Ben then asked our ministry for advice. Our bishop said, "You don't want your son to be treated like a guinea pig. I'd just keep him at home, take his cast off, and enjoy family time together."

Mervin enjoyed the gifts that friends gave. We have a picture of him playing on the floor, pushing a wooden log truck, while wearing his sweetest smile.

As time went by, Mervin's toes that were sticking out from his cast became a little blue-looking. So Ben took his cast off. We felt a bit uneasy, but also felt the support of our church leaders. What a blessing to be part of a Christian church group, knowing that God's presence is with us.

We were doing all we could for Mervin's health. We tried different options. He was feeling good, and we tried to live a normal home life while enjoying every new day with our family of four. We knew that God could heal if it was His will but we couldn't think of giving up our blue-eyed, bond-haired, sweetest "smiley" boy. Mervin and two-year-old Nathan had a lot of nice times together, also their two sisters. We took Mervin on wagon rides to the barn.

Mervin's leg began swelling and the tumor was growing out from where the doctor had cut into his bone. We tried to keep him comfortable.

One day he was lying on his sofa-bed and asked, "Mommy,

what could I do for you?" He always enjoyed being a helper. So I gave him eggs to wipe clean. That made him so happy. After a while an egg broke, and he felt sad. I said, "That's all right." I felt sorry for him, cleaned it up, and gave him a kiss while praising him for doing his job well.

Mervin was the dearest, meekest, most kindhearted boy. He was easy to work with and always tried to please others. He enjoyed going to Sunday School even though he couldn't walk. Dad carried him down the steps to his classroom, but soon our going to church together ended. Mervin got weaker and his tumor grew.

One sunny day in April we got someone to make round bales out of corn fodder. Mervin was given a ride out the lane in the little wagon so he could watch the baler. The field next to the corn field was covered with dandelion flowers. Mervin said, with a smile, "If I could walk I'd get a little bucket and fill it with dandelion flowers." Life seemed so cruel to this four-year-old that would enjoy childlike freedom in life.

Mervin's tumor was a fast-growing one. There are no words to describe the condition of his leg. The skin broke, the tumor grew to the size of a large cabbage head and had a bad smell. It seemed as if the cancerous tumor grew on air. It was all spongy.

Thursday evening, April 29, I laid beside Mervin to put him to sleep. He helped me sing "Jesus Loves Me". That blessed my heart — to hear his weak, yet joyous voice coming forth! What precious memories... But Mervin was in pain. We were thankful for our family doctor's support in giving pain medication.

That evening I was so tired and went to bed after Mervin was asleep. But the night was interrupted because of Mervin's pain in his leg. He wanted Mommy by his side. He felt miserable!

Early Friday morning I laid on our bed, exhausted. Daddy went to Mervin's bedside. I prayed, "Our God, You promised that You wouldn't put more on us than we can bear. God, I can't bear it any longer! Your promises are true. Amen."

Just then I heard Mervin-dear calling. "Mommy!"

Daddy said, "Mommy is very tired." Thoughts came to me, *"What if he wants to say something for his last words."* So I went to our dear son, so frail, weak, and thin. He said he wanted to go outside. So I sat on his bed and held him. Before long, I felt his body being lifted up, and he fled away to Jesus! We cried, "Oh, he's gone!" With tears Daddy said, "He's not with us anymore."

The time was 5:15 a.m. and the date was April 30. We awakened our other dear children. Now life will be filled with "new" difficulties.

When the undertaker came, he carried dear Mervin's body down the steps in a white sheet. Eunice (6), Carolyn (5), Nathan (2), and Ben and I watched him go. Eunice, with tears in her eyes said, "I don't want them people to take Mervin!" We explained that it was just Mervin's body they were taking. His soul was with Jesus now. He's happy and singing with Jesus, Grandma Shertzer, and others. Yes, Ben's mother had died of cancer at thirty-five years of age on April 9, 1961, when Ben was only four years old. Now she can see her little four-year-old grandson who is the age her little boy was when she had to leave him and his two sisters, ages six and eleven.

The graveyard was appropriately covered with pretty yellow dandelion flowers. As the grave was being dug, we had memories of Mervin when he said, "If I could walk, I'd pick dandelion flowers and put them in a bucket." Dandelion flowers now have a special meaning to us. God made them special too!

May 4, we gathered together with family and friends for dear son Mervin's last tribute. Mervin's favorite song, "Jesus Loves Me", was sung at the funeral. Verse two was very touching: *"Jesus loves me, loves me still, though I'm very weak and ill, from his shining throne on high, comes to watch me when I die."* We also sang, "Silently They Pass Away" and "Jesus While Our Hearts Are Bleeding".

The following poem was read at Mervin's funeral.

The poem was composed as a tribute to Mervin Shertzer (age 4) who, the day before his passing asked his Mommy to come with him, and moments before death asked her to stay with him...

Come With Me

Mommy, stay with me, the pain is so strong.
Please help me, Mommy, to sing that sweet song
O how Jesus loves me, even when I am low,
Yes, Jesus loves me, His Word tells me so.

Mommy, come with me, hold my hand as I go,
You've taken good care, and I do love you so.
As I go to heaven, I want you along,
Together as here, we'll sing heaven's song.

Daddy, come with me, your strong arms have borne
Us all through my illness,
though your heart has been torn.
You've struggled with questions, now I only can say,
I want you to be with me to share heaven's day.

Come along, brother, sister, we've shared many hours,
We've played church and farming
through sunshine and showers.

I can't think of heaven without you being there.
Don't fail in the journey, there's so much to share.

Grandpas and Grandmas, come along with me, too,
Don't let life's involvements obscure that bright view.
Though we've moved far away, you've still had my love,
And I want you to share in my joy up above.

Uncles and aunts, look heavenward,
  along with cousins and friends,
Make sure you are coming with me,
  where friendships shall never end.
We've traveled together in life for a short enjoyable time,
I'll be waiting over yonder for you,
  to share in the glory sublime.

To all who are conscious that God
  has moved in calling me home,
Prepare today for your future,
  when no longer in this life you will roam.
Whether few days or many, it's all so soon spent.
When your life is over, will folks know where you went?

—David Wadel

As the days went by it seemed that the world must stop but we had to keep going. Heaven is closer since we started a home there.

Soon after Mervin's parting, I went to his bedroom. Beside his bed on the floor I found little fuzz-balls from his yellow stuffed duck. He pulled those fuzz-balls off and sucked thumb with them in his hand. I put those fuzz-balls in his memory book. The yellow duck and its little case are stored away in a box.

As I was lying across our bed one afternoon, I prayed that God would somehow reassure me that our dear little Mervin is in good hands with Jesus. I no longer could care for him. Then in a vision I saw Mervin and I holding hands and walking — oh, the transparent bridge with pure crystal-blue water beneath us. We were going up a path with a beautiful rainbow ahead when we came to a hill, and Mervin went over the ridge and disappeared. Oh, that was such a comfort to us. We knew that God cares about our hurts, and hears our requests. I thanked God for His love to us, in showing me this vision. That was just what we needed.

Ten months later, God sent us another gift. February 23, 1988 our prayer was answered. God blessed us with a precious son whom we named Melvin, (named after Mervin). We had prayed that God would grant us another son that looks like Mervin, and Melvin sure did! My mother said, "Are you sure that God didn't send Mervin back to you?!"

Once again we had a happy family of four children, all healthy and enjoying each other's presence. But we missed Mervin so badly! We lived with fond memories.

Time went on. Ten-year-old Eunice and nine-year-old Carolyn were going to school and enjoying life.

In the summer of 1993, I was washing dishes when Carolyn came to me and said, "Mommy, look at my leg. I have a bump." It was a small, but very hard, lump on her left leg two inches below her knee on the bone.

I tried not to worry, but thoughts of Mervin's leg came to my mind. "We'll have to keep watch on it," was my reply. Carolyn said it didn't hurt. (It was only four years since Mervin had died.)

As the days passed by, Carolyn's lump grew larger, became

cone-shaped and hard as bone! We tried to work with it at home, but we finally took her to our family doctors. They were concerned and took x-rays. That made us feel uneasy again. Prayers were sent to our caring God.

The doctors sent us to the Geisinger Hospital for more tests. Dear Carolyn had to go through a lot of fear for a nine-year-old child! We tried to comfort her by being close by her side. An MRI was again required. All we could do was submissively lay every thought and anxious fear upon our All-Knowing Creator. He promised to carry us through all the trials of life, and we felt His presence now.

After the tests came back, the doctors leaned heavy upon the thought that it appears to be similar as to what our son Mervin had. But they also want a biopsy done to check what kind of bone tumor it was!

So Carolyn tried to be brave as she got ready to undergo anesthesia. It wasn't easy for us to face all the unpleasantness of tubes, needles, and a surgery gown for our sweet girl. Tears just flowed down our cheeks, but we tried not to let Carolyn see them. Then our dear, precious girl was taken through the doors on a bed to the operating room. Ben and I were left alone on the other side of the closed doors. We embraced each other and wept while asking God to be near to Carolyn and to keep her safe.

We were so thankful to have each other while facing these hard circumstances. Ben and I depended on each other a lot. After a while we were allowed to be with Carolyn again. She was placed on a wheel chair, and was in much pain.

The doctors told us that Carolyn's bone tumor was the same kind as Mervin's, but this one was slow-growing. They thought since she was free from cancer elsewhere in her body, they could cut out the tumor and the bone would mend itself. We were so thankful to hear that. But they also wanted to give her chemotherapy for a year. That brought to our minds how it would change our home life. The doctor let us go home, saying he would talk things over with the other doctors.

The next day the phone rang. Ben was talking to the doctor. I heard him say "amputation" — all our strength left us. Poor Carolyn has to lose a leg! Then Ben told the doctor he wanted a second opinion.

The following days were very stressful. The doctors let us have the x-rays. Then friends advised us to try for a second opinion in a Mexico hospital. So we prayerfully made arrangements for a three-week stay in Mexico. That wasn't easy — to leave our three young children. Melvin was only two years old. We were thankful for family, church friends, and neighbors to help out at home. Ben's parents stayed with the children. A few boys from church did the milking and others helped with various other barn chores. In times like these we felt so unworthy of others' love and support, but most of all, the many prayers ascending in behalf of our overwhelming trials.

After spending three weeks in Mexico under their treatments for Carolyn, it seemed her tumor wasn't getting smaller. So with heavy hearts we knew that something else *had* to be done. Carolyn spent her tenth birthday in Mexico on October 5, 1991.

We said good-bye to others that were facing life-threatening experiences in Mexico.

How anxious we were to see our dear, parentless children. As the plane was flying homeward during the dark night hours, I had to wonder how God looks down upon this world. Are there any souls taking time to pray to Him during the quiet night hours?

We had such mixed feelings about poor Carolyn. What must she face in the medical field?

It was so good to be back with our family of four children. We continued Carolyn's medication from Mexico for a few months.

December 13, 1991 was a day of memories. It would have been Mervin's ninth birthday and... Another tragedy happened!

Ben was helping our church group men put a new roof on our Sewing Circle building while the ladies were having Sewing Circle inside the building. After a while we heard a thud. One of the men came into the building and asked me to come out. Ben fell off the roof — slid off on a black sheet of paper. He had pain in his back. He was told to lie still on a blanket till the ambulance came.

Ben was taken to the hospital by ambulance with me sitting on the front passenger seat. I sensed the folks were concerned about me too, going through this experience, as I was expecting a baby before too long. Our minister and his wife, David & Orpha Kauffman, followed the ambulance. They were there to help wherever they could. That was comforting to us. I wasn't used to going ahead without my husband's support, and to fill out all the information at the emergency desk...

The x-ray showed that Ben had three fractured vertebras. They gave him a pain shot and he tried to do all in his power to act well enough so he could go home. And he *was* allowed to leave the hospital. Our minister and his wife took us home. Ben was thankful to enter the house, even though he had a lot of discomfort. We then put a hospital bed in the living room for him. I slept on the sofa close by as he was unable to help himself. I fed him and supported him as he walked the next few days. We received a Lazy

Boy recliner as a gift from our family, which was very much appreciated. Ben used it a lot during these days. We also borrowed a wheel chair from our neighbor.

It seemed that the prayers of the many people had blessed Ben with fast healing. After a few weeks, I wheeled him out to the barn with the wheel chair. He was anxious to see things at the barn. Again, we had to be at the receiving end while others helped us out, doing our chores, etc. What would we do without the support of our church group? What a blessing!

When Carolyn was in the third grade, she was feeling well and had no pain in her leg, but the bone tumor was still growing! Ben was back to his normal work. We valued our health tremendously.

January 25, 1991, another healthy, precious daughter was granted to us. We named her Sharon Louise. What a blessing she was to the family, especially to the older girls: Eunice (11) and Carolyn (10). They had Nathan and Melvin but how they wished for a baby sister?

We were enjoying our family ties and counted each day a blessing before Carolyn would have to face the medical doctors again. That time came soon enough. When Sharon was four weeks old, we felt the pressure of the doctors to start Carolyn on chemotherapy treatments.

The doctors and nurses tried to do all they could to help us through Carolyn's treatments. They wanted to give her four months of chemotherapy. Next they would amputate her leg at the knee, then administer eight more months of chemotherapy. That made us so sad. If only God would grant healing and take away all our stress, but our ways are far from God's ways! He has a purpose for each one's life — to use us for His honor and glory.

We were not ready for the day when Carolyn had to face

the anesthesia doctors again. They put a medication-port on the side of her chest under the skin and attached a tube to her main blood vein at her neck. It was all under the skin. This was done to administer chemotherapy treatments in order to prevent always trying to find a vein and pricking her for each individual treatment. Without the port, her veins wouldn't have been able to hold up for all the strong chemotherapy.

Carolyn's treatments in the hospital consisted of five days a week, then off a week, back on three or four days, then off a week, to be repeated for one whole year. She had a rough time at the beginning of the treatments. She was smitten with nausea and vomiting. We were so thankful for Zofan, the new drug, that came out to prevent vomiting. She was a sick girl when we took her home for a break. But as soon as she felt better, it was time for another treatment. Home was such a special place to us!

The hospital became our second home during our lengthy stay. The grandparents stayed with our other children while Carolyn, baby Sharon, and I had to face hospital life.

We had the nicest chemotherapy doctor, and the nurses showed a deep interest in us too. They were impressed with Carolyn's quiet behavior and happy smiles. They also enjoyed holding a "healthy" baby in the hospital. They would take Sharon from her crib and hold her.

In the turmoil of our thoughts, we were hoping Jesus would return before June 9 so Carolyn wouldn't need to face amputation. That thought was too overwhelming for our minds. Our nights were often spent in prayer.

June 9, 1992, baby Sharon, dear Carolyn, and Ben and I traveled the fifty miles to the hospital to face this hard experience — making Carolyn a handicap for the rest of her life! By faith, we hoped this would save her life by keeping the cancer from spreading to other parts of her body.

Again, Carolyn was in the hospital bed. The nurses were getting her ready for the amputation in the pre-operating room. Ben and I were by her side and baby Sharon was sitting on Carolyn's bed.

We don't know what all went through dear Carolyn's mind but she tried to brave her tender feelings. Just before she was wheeled away, the anesthesia doctor gave her medication in the vein to make her feel sleepy. We gave her a kiss and tried to comfort her by saying, "Jesus will be with you." Tears flowed down her face. Oh, how hard it was for us to see our own flesh and blood, dear Carolyn, being taken away from us, knowing that this would be the last time we would see her with two legs.

With tears and praying thoughts, we waited in the waiting room for two-and-one-half hours. Then the doctor came to us and said, "Carolyn is through with her surgery and everything went well."

We longed to see our precious girl again. But, oh, she looked like she went though a lot. A cast was on the stump, which was all that remained of her left leg! We were pleased to hear the doctor say that he didn't need to cut her leg bone. He just removed her kneecap and took away the bottom part of her leg at the knee, hoping to promote faster healing.

Carolyn was allowed to return home again with a walker and crutches the day after surgery. Now Carolyn used Daddy's recliner. The mailman brought cheer when Carolyn received mail from caring friends and family. She also received a few sunshine boxes. Opening a gift each day brightened her days while she just sat...

After a few days at home, her stump was so swollen that

Daddy called the doctor. So Carolyn was again returned to the hospital to take off the cast and dress the stump with a soft dressing. That sounded great. We were one step closer to healing! Carolyn did very well as she watched the doctor run the saw around her cast, then lifted the top half off. We saw the very sore, red, swollen stump. The stump was bandaged and we went home.

Carolyn was allowed a few weeks at home for healing, then eight more months of chemotherapy followed.

Carolyn's life had changed. It was hard for her to think that she can't ride bike. But she kept up her courage and willing mind to accept her handicap for life, and kept going as normal as possible. She sat on the air-tire wagon and pushed the wagon with her one, and only, leg. Then one day she said, "Mom, let's go the Bargain Barn and get a three-wheeler so I can drive that."

"What if there isn't one there?" I asked.

She bravely said, "I know there is one there. I can see it right now!" So after asking Daddy, we left. And to our surprise, there was one there!

I had to think of the faith of a child. I felt so touched that God had allowed Carolyn's wishes and faith to be experienced. God's love is kind. He careth about us, and all His children.

Carolyn experienced much joy in riding this little plastic three-wheeler. She would use her hand and her leg to pedal it. She enjoyed her time at home between chemotherapy treatments playing with her sisters, Eunice (11) and baby Sharon, also her two brothers, Nathan and Melvin.

Carolyn was fitted with an artificial leg and made out wonderfully with it.

Carolyn lost her hair faster than we had expected in the beginning of her treatments. We felt so sorry for her to go to school without hair. She left her light hooded jacket on during school. We soon got her a hair replacement with long hair. She did great at keeping up with her school lessons at the hospital, at home, and at school between treatments.

The year of treatments slowly, but surely, crept on. Dad came to see us almost every day at the hospital. Carolyn was hooked up with an I-V pole. So she would go to the window to watch Daddy drive into the parking lot and find a parking spot. We were so anxious to see Nathan and Melvin get out of the car with Daddy — what a comfort to see them again. Eunice had to be in school without her dear sister Carolyn. Sharon was in her walker and learned to walk in the hospital. Having baby Sharon with us in the hospital for her first year of life brought a lot of joy to Carolyn and me. She kept our minds occupied.

November 25, 1995 was our seventeenth wedding anniversary. We also welcomed our seventh child that day, another healthy baby son who weighed five pounds and was born six weeks early. But everything went well with the delivery at the midwife's home. We felt God's love and mercy extended to us again. We named him after his daddy, Benjamin Edward, in keeping of the tradition of using the name Benjamin for the sixth generation. Since he was born prematurely, he just slept. I had to feed him every few hours, day and night. I felt exhausted! Then he took off and started to gain weight. At six weeks he contracted RSV (a severe cold) and was hospitalized for three days. Thankfully, he is a healthy boy today.

We did not know the future, but this was to be our family's largest number though only for a short time. With dear Mervin in heaven, we didn't take our children for granted. Each one was special and dear to our hearts.

The following was written by Melvin for a school assignment in the second grade.

I wonder about many things. I wonder if Jesus is coming today. I wonder how God can make so many snowflakes and how many days we will need to stay home from school. I wonder how God can keep track of how many hairs I have on my head. I wonder how old I will live to be.

I know there is somebody that never wonders. It is God!

—Melvin, age 8 (1995 - 1996 School term)

God knew the future for Melvin. This writing is now very dear to our hearts!

May 22, 1997, our attention was drawn to Melvin (9). His left leg was swung outward when he was walking. Earlier he had headaches but we attributed it to his asthma problems.

Carolyn, Nathan and Melvin were going to school for the few last days before summer vacation. We were looking forward to a good, happy family time in the summer months. But with Melvin's uncertain health problem, a dark cloud hung over our "happy" thoughts. As days went by, his unusual way of walking became more noticeable, and frequent headaches plagued him. As I was putting the school lunch boxes away for the season, my thoughts wandered. *"What will the future hold till we use these lunch boxes again?"*

We took Melvin to our family doctor, and he sent us to the hospital. We again had to face a lot of tests and an MRI for dear Melvin. When the specialist talked to us, he first leaned toward a possible stroke. But seeing the test results, he said, "This is altogether different than what I thought.

It's bad, very bad. A brain tumor is what we found, and it's malignant — inoperable."

What a blow?! I thought, *"Must we give up our dear Melvin too!"* I felt like fainting, so the nurses brought a chair and a cup of water for me. The doctor went on to say, "The tumor is in the center of the brain which affects his nerves and muscles." His left side was limited. He couldn't use his left arm. He stayed in the hospital for a few days while they placed a shunt in his head to drain the excess fluid from his brain. The tube, or shunt, drained from his head to his intestinal cavity. This procedure stopped all his headaches.

Melvin was so sweet through all this. He continued to do things, even though he was limited to using only one arm. Daddy made a birdhouse for Melvin and he painted it. He would pick flowers and bring them to me with his sweet smile radiating his face.

A few weeks later, June 26, the incision was healed, so they started chemotherapy treatment. He had seven treatments in a nine-week period of time. The new MRI showed that his tumor had doubled in size, even during chemotherapy treatments. Then the doctors recommended radiation treatments.

September 8, Melvin began with radiation treatments which consisted of five days per week for five weeks. We were disappointed when told that he must have anesthesia daily because he can't lie still enough for treatment. We were allowed to be with him when they gave the first anesthetic. Oh, our hearts were torn to see our son struggle till he was asleep. Since the tumor had affected Melvin's muscles and nerves, they increased the amount of anesthetic to relax his reflexes.

After he was in recovery, the doctors came and talked to us, asking if we would allow them to put a broviac line in him since his veins would be difficult to find for daily anesthesia. They said it would be just a minor surgery, lasting one-half to three-fourth's of an hour, but it sounded scarey. They would put a tube from Melvin's collar bone to his heart vein. They proceeded with the surgery since the tubes were all hooked up yet. We told the doctor about it being our third child with cancer. "Please take good care of our son," we shared with tears. Hours went by... We couldn't sit any longer while wondering what the doctors are doing to our dear Melvin. We *tried* to rest in the Lord. Finally, a doctor called to the waiting room with an apology for taking so long. They had problems getting the tube in at the collar bone. We can hardly wait to see our dear son again. After sharing with a nurse of our son's experiences, and our past experiences with cancer in our other children, she cried and said she also had a five-year-old son who passed away with a brain defect. She was so touched that she let us go into the Recovery Room to be with Melvin.

How our longing eyes searched that room for Melvin. Oh, there he was! He was restless and tossing and coughing. The nurses asked if I wanted to hold him, but how — all those cords got wrapped around him. How good it was to hold him close while he calmed down somewhat.

Our other children were waiting for us to come home. That evening we had planned to have our church group help to dig our potato crop. We had planted six hundred fifty pounds seed potatoes.

Our two oldest girls were now fifteen and seventeen years old and had to do the milking besides caring for little Benjie who was almost two years old. We felt relaxed, knowing that their cousin, Henry Garman, was there to help with the chores.

When a brother from church brought us home from the

hospital, all the potatoes were dug!

That night Melvin was so sick. He didn't sleep all night. He was vomiting and very restless. His body quivered from the reaction of his nerves. The whole bed was vibrating. This was terrible. This boy needed sleep!

The radiologist said the treatments will probably help to shrink the tumor, which was the size of two walnuts, and take some pressure off Melvin's brain. The weakness in his left side could be lessened somewhat but he didn't think they could cure the brain tumor. At any rate it would be back again in four to six months. Ben asked whether we may stop the treatments if Melvin couldn't tolerate them. The doctor said we may, but he wanted to give him a chance, if possible.

Since Melvin had such bad effects with the first treatment, and the effects of the anesthesia was unreal, he was not allowed to eat after midnight and had to stay on clear liquids till 9:30 a.m. This would be a daily procedure. The poor boy couldn't eat, and the anesthesia made him vomit. Ben said, "Melvin can't take this." So after that first treatment, we decided to discontinue treatment right away.

As the tumor grew, Melvin's side vision was effected and he lost his balance. We got a wheelchair to give him rides to the barn. He was a quiet, patient, "smiley" boy and had no pain. What a blessing!

August 26, our school started with only half a day. Melvin was ready for fourth grade and wanted to go for a little while to see his friends. I stayed with him at school for one hour, then he got so tired that I took him home.

September 15, Melvin was feeling better. He had slept all night and ate well. We didn't know what God had planned for his life but committed him to His will.

October 1, Melvin's condition had deteriorated. He couldn't talk or swallow very well and started having seizures. When Melvin could still talk, he had mentioned that he wants to meet his little brother Mervin and Aunt Lydia in heaven.

October 6, Carolyn (15) was baptized. Melvin was carried into the church basement, and placed in the Nursery Room during services. He was helpless and unable to talk.

At home he sat on the recliner chair. His arm would constantly move back and forth due to the reaction of a nerve. Kindhearted Sharon tried to do things for him and fed him a few times. Melvin and Sharon had been best playmates before he took sick. Melvin used to enjoy making her laugh, which wasn't hard to do. Now life had changed for the two of them, and for the rest of the family too.

October 29, Melvin went into a coma, and his breathing seemed difficult. So Ben requested that the school children be brought home. We felt it might not be long till Melvin wouldn't be among our family circle upon this earth. We, as a family, *tried* to sing "Jesus Loves Me" to Melvin while he laid on the recliner. Soon his soul fled from his weak body.

While we waited for the undertaker, a few neighbor women stopped by — not knowing about Melvin's death — with broken hearts, they embraced me as we wept together. Surely God had sent them for this sad occasion.

We were told that the viewing and funeral consisted of over one thousand people from ten different states. Melvin's life had touched many lives!

For the funeral message we chose Melvin's favorite passage from the Bible, *"Come unto me, all ye that labor and are heavy laden, and I will give you rest" (Matthew 11:28).*

Four of Melvin's nine-year-old classmates and two of his

nine-year-old cousins will never forget being pallbearers for dear Melvin's funeral.

We have special memories of our two sons who are now together in heaven.

These are some of the songs that we sung at Melvin's funeral: "Let Me Go Where Saints are Going", "I Wonder, Often Wonder", and "I Need No Mansion".

Farewell, Classmate

Melvin came to school on the first day. In the morning he watched us play. After about an hour of school his mother took him home because he got tired.

On the 17th of September we sang for him. If we would bend down so that he could see our faces, he could remember our names.

On the 29th of September we started sending artificial flowers with butterfly notes home every day. Around the 13th of October we started to send other notes to him.

On October 29, we heard that Melvin died.

On November 3, we had off from school for his funeral.

Sister Esther, teacher, put a poem on the bulletin board with Bible verses around it. The title was "In Loving Memory of Melvin". There were also pictures of our happy times together.

In Loving Memory of Melvin

After he died, we started writing things we remember about him.

February 23rd would have been his 10th birthday, so his mother made a birthday cake that said, "In Loving Memory of Dear Melvin's 10th birthday". She brought it for us to eat at school.

In the hall now there is a display about Melvin. It says: Budded on earth to bloom in heaven. There is also a poem.

We miss him at school but we know that he is in heaven where we can meet him if we are faithful.

—Anthony Weaver, Grade 4

A few weeks after Melvin's passing, Sharon was sitting on the recliner and said, "Now I'm sitting on the sick chair. I'll be the next one to get sick!" I thought, "Why does she say that?" She was a healthy, chubby girl. I tried not to take it seriously, but her statement came true. I believe that God at times allows a forewarning in our lives to prepare us in some way for the future.

Our local news reporter published the following article after Melvin's death.

Ties That Bind

Chuck Wagner, Sentinel Reporter

The Shertzer family clings to its faith amid misfortune
Every salty tear lands at the base of a tree of strength.
And there is reason to weep.

Melvin, just 9 and a deep thinker who wrote down personal thoughts well beyond his years, died of a brain tumor in late October. His sister and inseparable companion Sharon, three years his junior, underwent surgery to remove a brain tumor one month later. Sister Carolyn, now 16, had a leg amputated at age 9 because of a tumor in the bone. Brother Mervin was stricken with bone marrow cancer and died in 1987, at age 4.

The eldest daughter Eunice, 17, son Nathan, 12, and Benjamin "Benjie", 2, have been spared the onslaught of cancer but have faced the loss of siblings.

Shackled to calamitous misfortune, the Shertzer family has turned the tide of tragedy into stronger familial bonds.

"It is certainly the Lord that gives us the strength to face it," says father Benjamin. "To be open about it helps. We have to share it to help lighten the load."

Unwavering honesty is part of the solution, the Mennonite family believes. The truth is painful, but no more so than the creeping inroads made when the inevitable is blanketed with deceit.

"Once it was clear that there would be no cure, we tried not to hide the reality with them," Benjamin recalls with both Mervin and, more recently, Melvin's downward slide from health.

"We told them about heaven and the beauty of it. We told them how wonderful heaven is," mother Ruth adds. "They never complained. They looked forward to meeting Jesus."

A constant reaffirmation of their faith keeps the family from nosediving into despair, yet there is still the desire to seek worldly answers to the family's endemic cancer.

"We've thought of a lot of possibilities. Really nothing seems to stand out: No high tension electrical wires, no dumps nearby," says Benjamin, rubbing the side of his face with one hand while sitting in his Oakland Mills' home. Radon, pesticides, toxicity — all conceivable environmental causes have been sought out and largely ruled out on their farm and greenhouse.

Genetics is a growing possibility. Doctors have drawn blood samples to test the parents' make-up. Researchers have linked a certain gene to the suppression of cancerous cell growth. Perhaps in a deficiency or aberration to this gene lies the source for the family's predisposition to tumors.

Cancer has cropped up over several generations on the

paternal family tree - Benjamin's mother died with breast cancer when he was 4 - but never in such an unmitigated fever of attacks.

"(The children) would know that they carry it. But there is nothing they can do," Benjamin says about the pending conclusions from the DNA test. Results which point to a genetic cause will do little in the way of consoling the Shertzers, who would have no recourse against their own DNA codes.

They find more peace in putting themselves in the hands of a Higher Authority and finding some value in their hard-won experiences that they can share with others.

All misfortune teaches lessons. Not always a positive lesson of what should be done, but often a negative lesson of what should not be taken for granted.

"Children are precious. They are a special gift." Benjamin says, clasping his hands together. His five children sit shoulder to shoulder on a bench across the kitchen table. They are quiet children, at least around strangers, and friendly and polite. "They are all very close to each other and the older ones help take care of the younger children when we need to take Sharon for her therapy," Ruth explains.

Both Benjamin and Ruth glow with appreciation for their children. And they are bursting with stories about the children that they seem eager to tell.

"Mervin loved to sing. He sang 'Jesus Loves Me' the night before he died," Ruth says, smiling as the memory echoes in her mind.

"Benjie (the 2-year-old) tells us all the time that Melvin is 'up with Jesus'," Benjamin recounts.

"The doctors all marveled at how well Sharon recovered from her operation. She was in the Intensive Care Unit for less than one day after they removed the brain tumor," Ruth

tells of the beaming girl at her arm. "They never had anyone recover so fast."

Sharon's flaxen hair is pulled over the long scar running up the back of her neck and skull. She smiles, and smiles, and smiles. And if you smile back, she wraps her arms around herself, drops her head, and grins.

There is little doubt that the children will never lack for nurturing in the Shertzer family. And the family had much spiritual help from its church group, which held a special prayer meeting the evening it heard of Sharon's diagnosis. Without health insurance, the family has also found its tightly knit association with the church a help on material fronts.

The Goodwill Mennonite School in Thompsontown has been a boon to morale for the younger children, and Sharon attends whenever possible, even if she shakes her head when asked whether the classroom is missed.

No one can guess what the future holds for this humble, and humbled family in Juniata County, but the thought of better days - even if other-worldly - is its life-line.

"It certainly doesn't help to give up. We have to keep courage. Life needs to go on. When it comes, it strikes like a blow. But there is nothing to do but go on," Benjamin says.

"We look forward to all being together in heaven," Ruth adds, pulling her daughter in close again.

Sharon

Jesus Lover of My Soul

November 20, 1997, just three weeks had passed since

Melvin's death and we were not ready for God to put us through another hard trauma.

Sharon (6) was in the first grade at school. She got sick and vomited in school. The next day she complained of a headache, had a fever, and vomited again.

We got concerned and Ben called the family doctor's office. It was Saturday evening so the nurse transferred us to our local hospital emergency room. Leaving our other children at home, we headed for the hospital. Sharon seemed very sick! (What will ever come out of this experience?) We called on God for mercy upon Sharon's illness.

The doctor checked her out and said her white cell count was high. He gave her antibiotics and told us, "She just has an infection. And since her brother had just passed away, it might also be a reaction of grieving. That's how children react sometimes." We knew that couldn't be true.

We took Sharon home and she had a miserable night. She held her head backwards and cried with pain in back of her head. Could she have spinal meningitis?

November 23, 1997, it was Sunday afternoon and as I was holding Sharon on the sofa, the phone rang. How it touched my weary mind to hear my sister's family and friends on the phone singing "God Will Take Care of You". I tried to reassure myself of that.

Tuesday afternoon, November 25, we took Sharon to our family doctor. He also tried to tell us that Sharon's reaction was how children sometimes grieved after a sibling's passing. We begged, "Can't we get a cat scan at the hospital to see if there is anything serious wrong?" So the doctor called to the local hospital and there was an opening almost right away. He asked us to leave his office and go straight to the hospital. Ben quickly called our minister, Laban, to meet us at our home. We would go with him to the hospital. We felt we needed some support during these uncertainties.

A nurse at the hospital took Sharon for the scan. She brought her back to us while she checked the test. She came out and said she wants to do the test over again. We asked if she saw something unusual. She said she did. What a blow again!

All our strength drained from us again. Did she see a tumor like Melvin's? *"Oh, God, please, have mercy!"* The x-ray was put in front of the light for us to see. The doctor said, "She has a brain tumor the size of a small lemon." Sharon was calm and sweet and had no pain at this time. "She needs to be Life Flighted to another hospital," came the unwelcome news. Ben asked to take her to Danville, as there they were familiar with our family history. Our doctor called the doctor at Danville, but they were persistent that we Life Flight Sharon! Ben and our minister, Laban, insisted they would drive her to the hospital.

We called home to let our other children know about dear Sharon and Eunice answered the phone. I told her, "Sharon has a brain tumor." Eunice then burst out with a wail, "Is she going to die too?" I quickly tried to comfort her by saying that Sharon's tumor is located on the bottom part of her head. It might not be as bad as Melvin's."

The news spread about Sharon's condition. Our church group had a special Prayer Meeting that evening at church. We felt the prayers of the saints ascending to God's throne in behalf of our painful tragedy.

Eunice called her Aunt Anna Mary to inform her of Sharon's illness. She was crying so hard that she could hardly talk.

Eunice and Carolyn, our two oldest daughters, had to face such unpleasant experiences far beyond their age in taking the home responsibilities without their parents! But the grace of God was near to all.

This same day was our nineteenth anniversary, also Benjie's second birthday.

November 28, Sharon had brain surgery. The doctors could only remove seventy-five per cent of the tumor.

After a few weeks Sharon was taken back to the hospital to have her stitches removed and for another MRI test. The results were miraculous! The test showed positive with no activity or trace of the tumor. However, the doctors wanted to start Sharon on chemotherapy and radiation treatments the next week, since the biopsy revealed that the tumor was a high grade, fast-growing cancer.

Sharon was given chemotherapy pills as an outpatient, also thirty-three radiation treatments. The radiation consisted of thirty daily treatments except weekends. It seemed like a mountain to climb. Church friends, neighbors, and family helped with the daily driving. The support during this time, was another blessing to add to the innumerable blessings we had already experienced.

We were trying to live a normal life and were thankful that Sharon was able to go back to school. Her cousin, Hope, helped her at school with her back lessons.

Carolyn was enjoying driving car, milking cows, unloading hay and helping in the greenhouse. We felt blessed, hoping life would be better lived because of our other trials. Sharon was almost finished with chemotherapy pills. She seemed to feel so good. Thankfully, she never lost her hair from the chemotherapy.

Carolyn's Faith Experienced Again

February, 1999, our dear eighteen-year-old Carolyn was again stricken with cancer. This time it was breast cancer. She took chemotherapy treatments as an outpatient, followed by surgery on April 20, 1999. It was a four-and-one-half hour surgery with two more hours in recovery. So we had a long, stressful day. Two days later she was back home again.

Carolyn was soon able to be back to her normal life. She and Eunice did baking for market: Pies, bread, whoopie pies, etc. The two sisters seemed to stick together in their enjoyable work talents.

Six weeks after Carolyn's breast surgery, she began thirty-three radiation treatments. Again we were thankful for the support of others to help us do the daily driving.

We experienced the strength and grace that was needed for Sharon's daily radiation. We had confidence that God's power wouldn't be limited as we faced dear Carolyn's treatments.

July 20, 1999, was Carolyn's last day of radiation. We had a busy summer, doing garden work, canning, freezing, and farm chores. By faith, we hoped all the family would be in good health from now on...

September 20, 1999, Sharon had a follow-up appointment at the hospital where they took a blood test. The next day the doctors also wanted to do a bone-marrow test — what a shock!

Three days later the doctor called and informed us that Sharon's blood and bone-marrow tests showed a lot of tissue in her blood.

Monday evening, September 27, the doctor called expressing concern about Sharon's blood count being too low. Now she needed blood transfusions. The next day she got one unit of blood. How sad — the chemotherapy had ruined her blood-marrow factor preventing it from producing healthy blood cells.

October 5, Carolyn had her nineteenth birthday. What a blessing to see our dear children being able to celebrate another year!

October 22, Sharon had to receive her second blood transfusion. Another bag of blood hung on the I-V pole, slowly dripping, dripping into her vein. This was repeated almost weekly.

October 29, this day two years ago was Melvin's death date — so fresh on our minds. We are so thankful that we didn't know the future. God only grants grace at the moment we need it.

December 13 was another day of memories. This would have been Mervin's seventeenth birthday. Our minds couldn't comprehend how special it would be to have a grown son to help on the farm!

We need to keep in mind — God makes no mistakes. Mervin is safe and happy in heaven. Heaven is our goal for our loved ones and us!

We spent our day at the hospital. Sharon needed blood again. We were so thankful that she was able to do these blood transfusions as an outpatient, so it didn't separate us from home life so much.

2000
A Year of Tragedy and Memories

January 6, 2000, Sharon got a brown puppy. Its front paws were white, so we named it Mittens. She enjoyed this small dog and always protected it from our larger dog. Sharon loved animals.

January 24, Sharon was in the hospital. The nurses said they didn't want her to be at the hospital on her birthday. An MRI test was taken and showed white spots where the brain tumor had been. That didn't sound very encouraging to our troubled minds.

January 25, Sharon celebrated her ninth birthday. She received a dolly high-chair and a tea set.

Sunday, January 30, we felt so privileged to have some of our hospital staff come for Sunday dinner. It snowed so much that the driving was difficult but they wanted to come. We gave our two chemotherapy doctors, and others, a horse and sleigh ride while enjoying showing them the farm. They also enjoyed seeing Sharon's puppies and bunnies. It was a very special day for all of us!

February 17, Sharon was in the hospital for her thirteenth blood transfusion, also a chest x-ray. She had a slight fever and the tests showed she had pneumonia in the upper portion of her right lung.

The worst news for Sharon was when the doctor said that she needed to be admitted to the hospital. She let the tears spill out and begged to go home. My heart felt like it was breaking for her, and the vacancy of home life without us... We called Daddy to inform him of the doctor's request. He talked to Sharon and tried to comfort her too. Our driver (a couple from church) left us behind and traveled homeward.

Saturday, February 19, the family was together at the hospital and Eunice stayed with Sharon while I went home with the other children. My heart was torn many-a-time while leaving the little ones at home. Also, the older ones needed Mother by their side when working, and to lift the spirits up during the uncertainties of life.

Monday Sharon was able to return home again!

Tuesday, February 22, Carolyn had to go to Elizabethtown to get her artificial leg lengthened. It was a blessing to see that Carolyn was growing and healthy.

Friday, when Sharon had her fourteenth blood transfusion and chest x-ray, the doctor asked Sharon about Mittens.

Sunday, February 27, Eunice and Carolyn were anxious to spend three weeks at Numidia Bible School. How special that the two sisters were able to go together. They even slept side-by-side on bunk beds. But their minds were at home, hoping that we were making out okay with the greenhouse and dairy work. Eunice and Carolyn enjoyed being together — not knowing the future and how short there joy would be in having each other.

While the girls were at Bible School, Sharon had a hospital appointment to start her on a new medication intended to build up her bone-marrow factor. Since the hospital wasn't too far from Numidia Bible School, we surprised the girls with a visit. We had mixed feelings.

March 22, Sharon was to our family doctor for to get her blood counts checked, then they sent the reports to the hospital. At 10:00 that night the doctor from the hospital called with concern about Sharon's low blood counts. We needed to arrive at the hospital early the next morning.

A driver from church took us to the hospital. When we got there a nurse took Sharon's temperature. Soon the doctors came into the room. They showed concern that

Sharon had a fever of 103 degrees. She didn't seem sick and was usually smiling. The doctor said she could have an infection and wanted to admit her again. He had warned us earlier that Sharon's condition could bring on some serious things. With her blood counts so low, she could start bleeding from her nose, resulting in death.

Soon the doctor came into the room again and stood at Sharon's bedside, looking at her with all seriousness, asked, "Sharon, do you sometimes think of Melvin? Where did Melvin go?"

Sharon replied, "To heaven!"

"Did you ever think of dying?" Sharon looked at him. The doctor said, "When I drive down the road, I sometimes think I could have an accident and die. But I don't always think about it. Do you pray to God to take your soul to heaven?"

Sharon quickly replied, "I pray evenings."

The doctor asked, "What do you pray about?"

Sharon shyly quoted, "Now I lay me down to sleep. I pray Thee Lord my soul to keep - if I should die before I wake, I pray Thee Lord my soul to take, but if I should live for other days, I pray Thee Lord to guide my ways!"

The doctor looked at Sharon with astonishment and replied, "That's amazing!"

Then the nurse brought a unit of blood and an antibiotic to put into Sharon's vein. While the blood was slowly dripping into her by I-V, she was seated on a wheelchair ready to go to the children's floor.

On the way to her room, Sharon saw a sign of "popcorn" for sale, so I bought a bag. The nurse took Sharon and I to the snack room where we watched the popcorn popping inside the bag in the microwave. It smelled so good! Then to our room we went, pushing the I-V pole and wheel chair, with a happy Sharon in it. She went home the next day.

Sharon enjoyed her days at home, playing with Benjie and Mittens. She also went to school between her hospital visits.

~

June 26

Disappointments Again — Sisters Facing Trials Together

Monday we took Sharon for a blood transfusion, and Carolyn went along due to a cough. Carolyn had a chest x-ray and bone scan done. As the tests were being taken, we prayed and prayed for dear Carolyn's life.

Soon enough we had to face the doctor with his reply, "Carolyn has cancer again — lung and bone cancer." He also said Carolyn and Sharon had fevers. I stayed with them at the hospital.

The following day, Tuesday, June the twenty-seventh, Carolyn had an x-ray done on her knee and hip. Sharon also had a chest x-ray. Carolyn got to go home, but her life had changed again. Eunice stayed with Sharon on Wednesday, and on Thursday Sharon was allowed to go home.

Friday, June 30, Carolyn was started on chemotherapy again. Sixteen months ago she had been healed from breast cancer. Her hair had grown back nicely. But now she would need to lose her hair again. We felt so sorry for her! Life surely doesn't seem fair in our eyes, but Carolyn had a submissive outlook again — holding onto faith to get well. Naturally she faced struggles, which any youth would, but especially now that her sister Eunice was dating Nathan

Yoder for the past year. Carolyn had thoughts about her close sister leaving home.

July 29, we got an invitation to a wedding in Georgia. With our concerns for our children, we were not sure that we should go. Carolyn seemed stabilized. We took Sharon to the hospital the day before we left so that she would have a full blood supply to keep her counts up till we came back home. The nurses thought she would do okay. They encouraged us to make the trip, thinking it may do us good to go. So Ben and I went with friends on a Greyhound Bus. Our minds went homeward, praying that all would go well. We called home when we arrived in Georgia, and again the next morning. We then went to the wedding and enjoyed the fellowship with friends.

Sunday morning Ben didn't think we would need to call home till evening. We went to Dublin Mennonite Church for the morning service. We were standing in line for a noon fellowship meal when the phone rang. Ben was asked to go to the phone. What a shock?! *Did something happen at home?* Our minds were immediately saddened with concern for our children.

It was Carolyn calling to say that Sharon was in the hospital and Eunice was staying with her. Sharon's nose started bleeding early Sunday morning and they couldn't stop it. Eunice had called our deacon, Brother Vernon, and asked him what to do. Should she call 911? He said she should.

The ambulance took Sharon to the local hospital where they plugged her nose. Sharon took it all well. But the doctors acted like they didn't quite know what to do since she was on chemotherapy. The local doctors called to our hospital at Danville wondering what they should do. The Danville doctors wanted her to come to them. They planned to transfer her by ambulance, but her bleeding had stopped. Brother Laban and Thelma had come to be with the girls at the hospital. Eunice expressed her thoughts that, "If Dad was here, he'd just drive her to Danville." So the doctors had Eunice sign a paper saying that if something happens, the medical personnel would not be held responsible.

So Laban drove really fast to the Danville hospital upon Eunice's request and faith. Upon arrival at the hospital, they started giving Sharon blood transfusions.

We, as parents, were so far away, but we could pray. We felt relaxed to know that Sharon was with our familiar, faithful Danville doctors. She would be in good hands.

With the help of our friends, they got us on a plane to fly home that same day. What a blessing and comfort to have friends of like-faith to help carry us through these uncertainties.

We arrived at Harrisburg Airport at 9:00 p.m. and we were at the hospital by 10:00 that evening. Thanks to family!

How anxious we were to see our dear Sharon, and the other children. They all seemed happy and Sharon was so glad to have us back.

Sharon was in the hospital the rest of the week because of pneumonia. We tried to do things to keep her occupied. One day three show dogs were brought into her room. That helped pass the time! Sharon also received special company when Uncle Stoners' and their children, on furlough from Guatemala, paid her a visit. While the visitors were there, a nurse came and requested to put a picc-line into Sharon's vein to save her veins from bursting. They needed to start some medication for her pneumonia. So our company had to step out of the room. A thin tube was inserted in her arm up to the neck vein. We felt so sorry for Sharon in all she had to face. She cried to go home! *"Why must life be so cruel for some?"* I pondered. The doctors discontinued the chemotherapy for her brain tumor while the pneumonia was being treated. After a week, Sharon went home with medication. Although, Sharon and Carolyn both went back for treatments in the Clinic as out-patients.

August 6, the Doctor took me aside and mentioned that Sharon's life was coming to an end. Her brain tumor was taking over since they discontinued chemotherapy. She could live a few weeks. I was burdened. How can we face death again? How can we give up our little girl? I felt so alone... But, God was nearby! Tears filled my eyes. Sharon vomited at the hospital due to her brain tumor. Her one eye had turned aside somewhat and she didn't have a full smile — signs of weakness from the tumor.

We were thankful to arrive at home, but sorry to share the news of Sharon's life to the rest of the family.

August 16, we went for another appointment at the hospital with Carolyn and Sharon. Carolyn had a lot of pain due to her bone cancer. Both girls needed to take treatments. Grandma and I were allowed to stay with them in the treatment room. Grandma Shertzer knitted booties for Sharon's doll while we waited till the treatments were finished.

Saturday, August 19, was another day we counted as a blessing to have Sharon still with us. Yet, she wasn't feeling the best and was vomiting again. We thought if she couldn't keep liquids down, she would dehydrate, so Ben called the doctor at the hospital. The doctor thought it would be best to bring her in. Sharon was weak and thin by this time. Ben carried her to the van. Benjie was nearby playing with Rydell (5), a neighbor girl, for whom we baby-sat at times. I called for Benjie to come give Sharon a good-bye kiss. "She might die," I told him softly. How sweetly they kissed each other good-bye... Then Rydell asked Sharon if she was allowed to play with her doll. Sharon wasn't sure — her favorite doll! I said, "May she if she takes good care of it?" Then Sharon said, "Yes," to Rydell. Our other children looked so sad to see us leave for the hospital again — not knowing if this would be their last good-byes to Sharon.

Sharon was lying down on the way to the hospital when she started to breathe heavy, and said, "My head." Ben and I became alarmed. Ben wondered if he should keep on driving. *"What if she dies?"*

Being burdened for Sharon in not letting her know that she would soon not be with us, I said, "Do you know you're very sick, Sharon, and may soon go to heaven? What for songs do you like if we if we would sing at your funeral?"

She thought a little, then said, "I don't want the same ones Melvin had."

At the hospital, Ben put Sharon on a wheelchair. After we were in her room, Ben went to park the van.

When I set Sharon on her bed, her face beamed as she said, "The song I want is 'Jesus Lover of My Soul', and 'Safe in the Arms of Jesus'."

I was shocked at her alertness and quick response. I thought, *"The Lord can still heal, if it's His will!"*

Soon Daddy came in and kissed Sharon. How we loved our girl — sick, thin, and pale. The doctor came into her room and said, "Oh, Sharon, my dear Sharon. You always have a smile. Even though you're sick, you don't act it. You're my best girl!"

The nurses brought in a bag of fluids and put a needle into her vein to draw blood. "My head!" Sharon cried out in pain. The tumor was putting pressure on her brain. They gave her pain medication and she soon fell asleep and we could no longer to talk to her. That night her breathing became labored. Later, we told the nurses how she was so still... Her breathing got quiet. *Was she in a coma?*

Soon the doors opened and the room was filled with doctors and nurses. They all wanted to check her out. They took chest x-rays, blood tests, blood pressure, checked her eyes, etc.

Then the doctor asked Ben to step outside in the hallway. He wants to talk to him. He said, "Sharon isn't going to be with us very long."

Ben asked, "May we call our children in?"

"Yes," replied the doctor.

Ben called our minister, Laban, at midnight asking if they would bring our children to the hospital. Words can't express how we felt.

Our children were awakened from their sleep and brought to the hospital at 2:00 in the morning. They looked so worried and frightened to see their dear sister lying unresponsive and laboring to breathe. They rested on the sofa and cot, but none could sleep.

Sunday, August 20, Labans left to attend Sunday morning church services. Eunice's special friend, Nathan Yoder, came to join the weary, sad family. My sister, Ella, also stayed with us instead of going to church. Later, more visitors came to show their support, and sang for us in the hallway.

Ben and I were standing at Sharon's bedside when she held her two hands up as if she was reaching. Shortly after that Sharon was carried into glory.

It was hard to gather our children together to go home, leaving our precious child's body behind. We were so thankful that Sharon wasn't suffering anymore. But, the empty van seat — and only four children with us for the drive home — it was overwhelming! We were glad that

Nathan Yoder drove the van home for us.

That night Carolyn missed her bed-partner, so she wanted Benjie to sleep with her. Eunice was also in the same room. As I was praying with the children in the girls' room, I was frightened to hear noise like wings flapping around me! I'll never forget the feelings I experienced at that moment.

Monday, August 21, the morning dawned as a beautiful, sunny day. We were startled to see how the sparrows flocked to Sharon's bird feeder at the kitchen window. Different times they flew against the windows. We never saw so many birds there at one time before. Was God sending us a message from Him of Sharon?

Getting preparations together for another funeral again so soon wasn't easy. It was just three years since Melvin's passing.

August 25, 2000, was Sharon's funeral day. We sang her two favorite songs: "Jesus Lover of My Soul", and "Safe in the Arms of Jesus". We also sang, "Farther Along" and "Tempted and Tried".

Our hearts and lives were experiencing a great loss — the loss of our dear Sharon. The memories of our two sons, Mervin and Melvin, were still so fresh on our minds. It was only God's love and grace that carried us through this sad occasion and the days and years ahead! How could we bear it alone? We needed the prayers — the comfort of others.

Brother David mentioned in his devotions that it was our loss and Sharon's gain. The funeral message was titled, "The Pearly Gates of Heaven," brought by Brother Laban. It was shared at the funeral that Sharon's cousin found in her autograph book what Sharon had written in 1998 when she was seven years old.

Dear Rhoda,

May the pearly gates of Heaven
Far across the crystal sea
Open wide someday Dear Rhoda
To welcome you and me.

Love your cousin,
Sharon Shertzler

Sharon's school teacher, Esther, had this poem on the bulletin board.

In Memory of Sharon

Our hearts are sad this morning
I seems a dreary day,
For Sharon will not come to school
God has called her away.

Our hearts are glad this morning
Though tears may dim our eyes,
It was God's plan that Sharon left,
His ways are always wise.

Sharon is forever enrolled
In her heavenly Teacher's care.
What wisdom now is hers,
Which man cannot compare.

She'll no more need the alphabet,
Or sounds a e i o u,
She has perfect knowledge from
The Alpha and Omega.

Sharon needs learn no more facts,
For God counts not by number.
She does not tire till end of day,
For there's no night nor slumber.

Sharon is busy adding
And multiplying too,
Her worship and love to God
Increases ages through.

What great anticipation
The first day of school brings
But we are glad in Sharon's joy
With supreme, heavenly things!

A friend of Sharon's wrote the following for a school assignment.

God's Way is Best

"God's way is best, I will not murmur / Although the end I may not see / Where'er He leads I'll meekly follow / God's way is best, is best for me."

God saw it was best to take Sharon to heaven three days before school started, August 20, 2000. Some of her last words that her family could understand were, "Safe in the arms of Jesus" and "Jesus lover of my soul".

The last thing she and I did together was peel cucumbers. "Good-bye, Joanna," were the last words she said to me! Once we were at their place again, she said that Melvin used to push her on the gate out in the barn. Then we *took turns pushing each other on it.*

She and I had dresses alike from our teacher, Debbie. Then Sharon's mother gave Sharon's dress to us after Sharon died.

I have many cards and gifts from her that I got ever since we were preschoolers. Some of the things she gave me are stickers, tablets, and a red cross. I still have a lot of the a lot of them.

We started school later this year, because of Sharon's viewing and funeral, August 24 and 25, 2000. On the west wall in our classroom we had "In Memory of Sharon" on the bulletin board, with a poem and two songs, "Jesus Lover of My Soul" and "Safe in the Arms of Jesus," and a few pictures of "Toy Day" and other things we as a classroom did together.

Out on the hall wall were papers shaped like books with one of the school students' name on each one. Around Sharon's book it said - Gone to bloom above, Life's book completed August 20, 2000, and some roses were on it.

We know that Sharon is having a much better time in heaven than she would have if she would be on the earth.

—Joanna Kreider (Grade 4)

Carolyn

"Good-night, I love you!" were the last words Carolyn shared with her father — just nine weeks after Sharon's death!

In the days after Sharon's passing, we claimed God's promises that He will never forsake us, and we keenly felt His love even though our hearts were hurting because of Sharon's absence. We had to face life with its responsibilities... And Carolyn had to continue with her hospital visits. It was hard to face the hospital where Sharon had died.

September 9, we celebrated my forty-fourth birthday by going with my brother and his family to Long Wood Gardens to enjoy the beauties of nature. Carolyn was in a wheelchair, because there was lots of walking. She enjoyed holding the little ones on her lap.

October 1, 2000, we had communion at church. It touched my heart to see Eunice and Carolyn washing feet together. That was one of the last "special" times they shared as sisters.

October 5, was Carolyn's nineteenth birthday. What a special day, and to see her feeling so well and helping with preparations for a special meal with a young family. Carolyn was so happy and sweet to all of us.

Carolyn's friend, Joanna, asked Carolyn to share something that was special to her, so the following song was what Carolyn gave her. Joanna framed it and presented it to her as a gift. Another friend also gave a wall-hanging with this song on it. We then sung this song at Carolyn's funeral.

There Is An Answer

So many questions that go unanswered,
Why pain and heartaches on ev'ry hand?
Who has the courage to keep on going?
Why all these troubles, who understands?

Yes, there'll be trials and tribulations;
More grace abounding to stand the test.
Just take up courage and keep on going
When life is over, eternal rest.

There is an answer for every question,
There are no secrets, our Savior sees.
He had the courage to keep on going
Up Calv'ry's mountain for you and me.

Our Savior left us this precious promise,
"If you'll be faithful until the end.
There waits in heaven a crown of glory;
And I'll be with you, I'll be your friend."

Someday in heaven there'll be no heartaches,
No pain or sorrow will e'er annoy.
There all our questions will all be answered,
When we see Jesus, Oh, perfect joy!

—Robert D. Toews

Reprint permission granted by poet. (This song is in *Precious Promises In Song No. 2* / Copyright 1990 by Prairie View Press)

October 16 — life had changed so quickly for Carolyn. Her lung and bone cancer grew so rapidly, and breathing was getting difficult. We took her to the hospital for a cat scan on her brain because the left side of her face had become paralyzed.

The doctors asked us to get oxygen started at home. We also got a hospital bed for Carolyn. She wasn't able to sleep without her head elevated. We got pain pills to ease her sore shoulders and back. Her bone cancer gave her much discomfort.

October 17, Carolyn went to the hospital to get set up for radiation. But she wasn't able to lie down for the radiation markings because she couldn't get enough oxygen when lying low. So, to Carolyn's disappointment, the nurses weren't able to accomplish her wishes. We had to leave the hospital without any hope of cure for our dear Carolyn, but she continued on faithfully with other options. She strived to get well!

Tuesday morning, October 17, I was pondering on Carolyn's short life... While she was sitting on the sofa I gave her a Bible, a piece of paper and pen, and asked her if she had any special Bible verses that were dear to her.

Then I went out to hang up a load of wash. When returning to her side, I was surprised to see how well she wrote out a few verses. I was expecting only the references to be written down. Carolyn had written this: *Revelations 22:12 "And behold I come quickly and my reward is with me, to give every man according as his work shall be." Verse 14, "Blessed are they that do his commandments that they may have right to the tree of life, and may enter in through the gates into the city."*

These verses must have been comforting to Carolyn. She had underlined a few of the words that were especially meaningful to her.

Carolyn had difficulty sleeping, so the doctor said to give her sleeping pills and pain pills.

October 19, she was able to breathe easier again after having been on oxygen for a few days. In the evening, Carolyn went into a deep sleep. Her breathing was becoming more labored. We thought she might have slipped into a coma. Maybe her time would soon be here to depart from this life.

We called Ben's brother and family to help us finish the evening chores. Later, they were at Carolyn's bedside with our family. Carolyn seemed so low. She was laboring to breathe and non-responsive.

After a while, to our surprise, she opened her eyes and said, "I hear singing! Why is the room so BRIGHT?!" She must have seen a heavenly vision! That was a comfort to us.

Friday, October 20, we were mindful that God's mercies are new every day. It was a beautiful, sunny day. Carolyn felt some better. She sat on the wheelchair outside enjoying the fresh air and warm sunshine. She also joined us at the table for mealtime in her wheelchair. Then to my surprise, she rinsed a few dishes. That was special. Carolyn always enjoyed being by my side, working and sharing conversation, even when she was well. She was such a helpful, tenderhearted, loveable girl — so unselfish.

Saturday morning, October 21, we felt blessed to have Carolyn with us for another day. A phone call revealed that a former friend from Lancaster County felt moved to "go see Carolyn" that day yet and he needed directions to our place.

He was an older man who had faced some dark times and hard trials in his life. He took the opportunity to share with Carolyn one last time as he sang songs to express his sympathy. It was encouraging for him to sing for others.

Some couples from church also shared their interest, and the ministry kept close ties with our lot in this experience.

Saturday night our family was weary. I was exhausted and fell asleep so I'd be able to take care of Carolyn during the night. Ben made a cup of tea for Carolyn and helped her with her pain pills and sleeping pills. Carolyn showed her appreciation for her father by saying, "Good-night. I love you!"

Later, I awoke to check on Carolyn. She was not responding. She was in a coma!

Sunday morning, October 22, 2002, Carolyn was facing death. Her body was so weak and her breathing became shorter. We called our neighbors to help do the chores. Then my brother's family and Nathan Yoder came to our house instead of going to church.

Sunday forenoon at 11:30, Carolyn dear was carried to heaven through the gates into the city, meeting her Lord and loved ones.

Ben called to the church to share the news of Carolyn's passing. He also called the grandparents and family.

Now our troubled thoughts had to change while focusing on a different outlook on life.

Carolyn was no more with us. Oh, how can we bear the emptiness she left? Now Eunice must go through life with no sisters — only memories of her sisters.

What a feeling it was when the undertaker arrived to carry away our dear, precious Carolyn's body. A neighboring friend came to share his sympathy upon hearing the news of Carolyn. Again, we felt God's timing as the neighbor was there to help carry Carolyn's body down the stairway in a white sheet zipper-case. I had to think that small body with just "1" leg, how it had to go through so much in this life! We don't understand God's ways.

The undertaker asked for Carolyn's clothing for the funeral. I was so thankful to call on Eunice to help me gather Carolyn's clothes. Eunice and Carolyn could wear each other's clothes. As Eunice was walking ahead of me to their bedroom, I felt a sense of relief to know that I still have one daughter and we shared such a close bond as Mother and daughter. Brother Laban's (my sister's family) and another family arrived as the undertaker was placing Carolyn's body in the funeral car.

Monday, the ministers came to make preparations for the funeral. We felt so sad, we could hardly help or share much. We had just faced Sharon's funeral plans nine weeks ago. We experienced strength and courage that came only from the Lord, not of ourselves. The viewing was planned for Thursday and the funeral on Friday, October 27, 2000.

Brother Noah brought out in his devotions, only *"if we're absent in the body can we be present with the Lord"*. He also expressed what Carolyn had to face in life — to see her brothers and sister suffering. Carolyn was five years old when Mervin died — when Melvin died, she was 16 years old — when Sharon died, she was almost 19. How concerned she was. How she hurt for the family. Carolyn probably wondered how they would face another death, and make out without her?

Brother Laban brought the message from Carolyn's verses which she had written only four days before her death. Revelations 22:12 & 14. He titled his message, "The Obedience According to Enter into Heaven". We really appreciated the message. The songs that were sung were, "If on a Quiet Sea", "Tempted and Tried", and "There is an Answer". The following poem was read at Carolyn's funeral.

To the Shertzer Family

A glad day 'twas when you were wed
November twenty-five
The year of nineteen seventy-eight.
To serve Him you did strive.

You knew God led your lives thus far
Content you followed Him.
Assured the Lord would give you strength
Your light need not grow dim.

With hearts rejoicing in His will
You welcomed Eunice dear.
Then Carolyn came to bless your home
It was in the next year.

Then to your home a son was born
December '82.
You named him Mervin; you felt blessed.
This son God gave to you.

But then a few years did pass by
And Mervin sick did lay.
'Twas April then of '87
When God called him away.

In nineteen eighty-five, I see,
Was born another son.
He answers when you call, "Nathan".
Your hearts I'm sure, he won.

Then Melvin joined your family
The spring of '88.
It seemed to help to heal the wound
That still was on the "slate".

In August of last year, my friends,
Another "blow" was brought
Into your lives. Dear Carolyn–
"Cancer" was what they thought.

Sometimes it seems like suffering
And trials more and more
Are brought into our lives, and yet
We know not what's in store.

The day of miracles, my friends,
Has never ended yet.
We know not what the future holds.
God would the glory get.

Another daughter brought you joy.
Sharon, I'm sure, is dear.
And may you as a family
Serve Him as you are here.

Then in November '95
Benjie the sixth was born.
It seemed like now your joy was full
In place of thought forlorn.

Then to your lives that dreadful plague
Came stealing swift and sure.
Your Melvin dear had cancer
For such there was no cure.

You watched in weakness in God's strength
As weaker still he grew,
Till in October '97
To heaven his spirit flew.

The stabbing pain of Melvin's death
Was so fresh on your mind,
When Sharon dear was taken ill.
Dear God, what will they find?

Cancer again! In faith you prayed
That healing would be wrought,
Till in August '2000 He called her home
Gave health beyond man's thought.

Meanwhile dear Carolyn's cancer raged,
Yet God was in control,
And though her body weaker grew
It could not mar her soul.

She stood with steadfast faith in God,
His Word was her chief joy,
Till nine weeks after Sharon's death,
Heaven did her praise employ.

So may our Heav'nly Father bless
Your home with special grace.
May you continue as you live
To look into His face.

For when the burdens and the cares
Are pressing down on you,
Remember there are friends who care
And they are praying, too.

—Mary Rohrer & Thelma Kauffman

Life must go on till we meet our Creator and Lord.

We appreciated all the support of the church, family, friends and neighbors during these hurting times.

As our children were facing cancer, and then passed away, our only hope was to look to Christ. What comfort we held to as we meditated on those "faithful Bible characters that God loved". Job's life, and others too... How He used them to bring glory to Himself! Yes, we felt His love.

In II Corinthians 12, we read, *"My grace is sufficient for thee, for my strength is made perfect in weakness."*

Philippians 3:13b says, *"... reaching forth unto those things which are before."* Verse 14 reads, *"Press toward the mark for the prize of the high calling of God in Christ Jesus."*

On September 8, 2001, God blessed our family to experience the wedding of daughter Eunice and Nathan Yoder.

September 10, 2002, we experienced the joy of becoming grandparents to a granddaughter, Lynnette Elaine. Nathans live in Belleville, Pennsylvania, only one-half hour from our home. We both attend Goodwill (Eastern) Mennonite Church.

Our three children's ages at the time of this writing are: Eunice (22), Nathan (18) helps us and neighbors with farm work, and Benjie is seven years old and in first grade.

After Carolyn's passing, a singing tape was published in Memory of Carolyn and her brothers and sister by Carolyn's Bible School friends and cousins. We treasure it a lot. We also have many memories of gifts given to our children, and the caring thoughts of cards, scrapbooks, and kind deeds shown during our many trials. For this we cannot be thankful enough.

—Benjamin & Ruth Shertzer
Oakland Mills, Pennsylvania

Clifford Ebersole

December 3, 1984 to January 16, 2001

Michael Ebersole

February 2, 1991 to February 17, 2001

In Loving Memory
Julia Ebersole, Mother

It was a foggy Monday morning, January 15, 2001, as twenty-year-old Julene left to teach school at Antrim where she was substitute teaching. The regular teacher was at Numidia Bible School for three weeks. Nathan, my husband, left for the diesel shop where he was working for only a short time.

We had decided seventeen-year-old Leslie should take the children to school. Our mini-van needed fixing so we were using our old station wagon to haul school children. This vehicle was not liked too well by any of the children.

Jokingly, Clifford, who just turned sixteen, said he is afraid he will have to take this vehicle to get his driver's permit.

Kevin, our oldest, was twenty-one and worked full time for a farmer from our church.

We have a dairy farm so there was plenty of work for our six boys. Kevin helped out evenings occasionally and Saturdays. Leslie was home and saw to the feeding and kept things going the days Nathan was at work. Clifford (16), Chris (13), Stanley (11), and Michael (10) were all in school. We were blessed with three daughters, Julene (20) at age sixteen she finally got a little sister, Glenda, then two years later baby Loretta arrived. Three-year-old Glenda and one-year-old Loretta were dearly loved by everyone, but were Michael's special little playmates even if they were six and eight years younger than him.

I had an extra busy day of washing clothes that day since Leslie had just come home from Numidia Bible School Friday night and I hadn't done any of his wash Saturday. How little we knew that Friday night, going to the closing program and bringing Leslie home, would be the last special thing we would do with our whole family. The memory of seeing our dear son walk with a limp into that full auditorium would linger with us, as well as be the memory for many others, for the rest of our lives.

Leslie was cleaning out heifer pens most of the day. In the afternoon I put Glenda and Loretta in bed for naps and let Leslie know so that he could check on them occasionally. Then I left to get the school children. The children were waiting for me when I pulled in at school. Clifford usually sat in the front seat but he had a box to put in the car, so he said, "I'll sit here," and sat in the back seat. As soon as Clifford got in I saw something was wrong. It went through my mind that his face looked like it did when he broke his leg. I asked him what was wrong. He answered with a big sigh, "I don't feel good. My head hurts and I'm so cold!" I thought, *"Oh no, he must be coming down with the flu."*

We didn't go far until he said, "Hurry home, Mom!"

I answered, "I'm sorry, Clifford, but I must stop and fill up with gas on the way home." He didn't say another word the whole way home but we would hear him sigh every now and then. Oh how I pitied him! I longed to make him more comfortable. He had told me that he had taken Tylenol at school, but I thought that he should take some more after we were home. He went straight to bed and I told the other boys that they had better start doing the evening chores right away because I didn't think Clifford would be helping.

After the boys went out, I went up to Clifford with water and Tylenol. He said that he could take them. I asked him if his head still hurts. "Yes," he said, "and I hurt so bad all over." I asked if it was anything like he had felt before and he said, "No, it's different." I left him then and went to get some supper on, but my mind was mostly with Clifford. I just had to think, *"Why, oh why, must Clifford suffer so much?"* He looked like he felt so miserable!

My mind went back to November of 1989. Two weeks before Clifford was five, he had fallen into a running blower. Nathan was unloading the last load of silage into the silo when I had looked out our kitchen window and saw Clifford at the back of the silage wagon watching it unload. He was not supposed to go on the side of the wagon towards the blower but we believe that he, forgetting all that and seeing that the load was almost empty, wanted to retrieve one last corn cob to eat the kernels off before they all went up the silo. So thinking, he ran up along side of the wagon and Nathan never saw him until Clifford was falling headfirst into the blower. There was a pile of spilled silage that he ran up on — maybe he missed his footing. He was pinched and held in an eight-inch area, just before the blower fan that blew the feed up the pipe into the silo. We believe that he was miraculously saved.

Nathan, with the help of a neighbor man, gently got him out and had him lying on the grass when the ambulance got to our place.

Clifford was taken to our local hospital, then air-lifted to York. From there he was again air-lifted in the "Life Line" to Hershey Medical Center where he was in surgery from 9:00 p.m. until 6:00 a.m. He had ten fractured bones, one compound brake in his left leg, and five large open wounds. He had no serious head or internal injuries. After two weeks at Hershey, he was brought to our local hospital by ambulance. He was there only one day and then came home. There was much suffering and many surgeries. Although this was very hard on the whole family, Clifford was endeared to each one of us in a special way. Amazingly soon he was up and around again.

One year later, and still in a cast, the left leg bone had not knit. Another surgery was done on his leg at our local hospital. A metal plate was put in and grafting was done. Six weeks later he was again at Hershey. They had found that he had bone infection and because the plate was foreign matter the infection became very active, deteriorating that bone to the size of a toothpick in just six weeks. Again, many surgeries followed but he was home within three weeks. The doctors let us know that there was only a 50-50 chance of healing.

Clifford was very cheerful and uncomplaining whenever he could be, and a very pleasant child to care for. There were times when the doctors considered amputating the leg, but at other times they weren't sure what should be done.

Our hearts swelled with thanksgiving to God when finally, after two-and-one-half years, his last cast came off and he was able to walk! Clifford was delighted to be able to wear two shoes again.

That leg started growing faster than the other one so he had a built-up shoe, but he did have his own special limp. We were still taking him to Hershey for follow-up, and it was uncertain what lay in the future. The large bone in his leg knit but the small bone never seemed to knit properly. This caused him pain many times. He only told me he had pain once it was very bad. I often could tell he had pain before he would say it by the way he would act, or by the look in his eyes. It seemed most of his life was lived in pain.

Coming back to the immediate care of Clifford, I decided to take his temperature and told him that I would be back to check him in a little bit. Well, when I went back to check him, the thermometer was on the floor, and he looked like he was sleeping. The thermometer read 103 degrees. I couldn't help but gaze at him for a while, hoping that he would soon feel better.

I was busy downstairs until around six o'clock when Clifford called me from the top of the stairs and asked me to bring a dishpan up because he threw up. I took one up and he said weakly, "You will have to clean the floor up over there. I couldn't get out of bed fast enough."

When Nathan came home from work, I told him, "Clifford won't be helping with the work. He is up in bed, sick."

"Well," Nathan said, " there is something going around. I sure don't feel good myself."

As I worked my mind was constantly on Clifford, and I'm not sure how many times I checked on him. He talked very little and had his eyes closed most of the time. Sometimes he lay like he was sleeping, and at other times he would be moving around a lot, seemingly very miserable.

Supper was eaten more quietly than normal because one was missing. As we gathered for family devotions, it was evident that Clifford was foremost in our minds as his name came up in our prayers. "Lord, would You heal Clifford if it is not against Thy will?"

Before I retired for the night, I once again tried getting Tylenol into Clifford. Once again I thought he was either sleeping, or perhaps didn't want to bother taking it because it wouldn't stay down anyway. I went to bed feeling uneasy — if only I could make Clifford feel more comfortable... Once again his name was brought to the Throne of Grace, and the household became quiet.

I was suddenly awakened by Leslie asking if I can't do something for Clifford. He said he can't sleep because Clifford keeps throwing up and is so restless. I told Leslie he could sleep downstairs, so that's what he did.

I was almost wringing my hands because I didn't know what to do for Clifford. For one thing he wasn't talking, telling me how he felt, or asking for anything to be done for him.

Kevin just had the flu and had been achy all over too. Before bedtime Kevin had mentioned about Clifford taking a warm bath as that had made him feel better when he was sick. I know Clifford did this twice in the night. I had asked him if it made him feel better and he said it did.

At 12:20 a.m., I checked Clifford again and he was more restless, almost whimpering at times and seemingly very uncomfortable. I breathed a constant prayer for God to be with him. I did ask him if he thinks he could drink a soda, then try to take Tylenol again. He said he thought he would try. I went and got the soda and a straw. When I returned to his bedside, he took a sip without lifting his head. I asked if he could take the Tylenol now but he had shut his eyes and never took it. Once again, I felt like I just had to stand there and watch him for a while. Feeling bad that I really didn't do anything to help him, I went and laid down but sleep wasn't there.

I went over again at around 1:20 a.m. and felt his head. It was cool and he looked more peaceful. I felt more at ease and did doze off when suddenly, around 2:00 o'clock, Nathan and I were both awake and Nathan said, "What was that?!"

I thought right away it was Clifford moaning. Nathan quickly went over, and running back said, "Quick! We must get him to the hospital!" Nathan saw Clifford sideways on his bed as if he just fell into it. He asked if he should take him to the doctor. Clifford's reply was, "Yes, you better Daddy, but I can't walk and I feel numb!"

Nathan quickly awoke Kevin to help with carrying Clifford, and I went over to Clifford to help get him ready. He sat up and I helped him into his clothes. As I was helping him, he said, "Hurry, Mom! Just put my socks on!" Of course, I assured him I was trying to hurry.

Kevin and Nathan carried Clifford downstairs and laid him on the table so I could wrap his coat around him. We all were hurrying as much as we could, thinking the most important thing was to get him to the hospital, quick! We still thought it was probably his high fever that was making him respond like this, and once he got help to get his fever down he would be okay.

Julene had to leave early for teaching at Antrim, so I

thought it would be better for Kevin and Nathan to go instead of me because he needed to be carried. Nathan also felt this was best. They left soon after 2:00 a.m.

Julene, Leslie, and I were all wide awake by this time and we knew sleep was out of the picture. We decided to have prayer together, asking God's protection over them as they traveled, giving the doctors wisdom, being near Clifford, and giving him health according to God's will. Also heavy on my heart was the thought, or prayer, to give Clifford's soul rest. Now we had turned it all over to God, but being human we waited to hear from Nathan with anxious hearts.

They laid Clifford on the back seat in the car and Kevin and Nathan sat in the front. As they were driving along, Nathan asked Clifford if there was anything they could do to make him more comfortable. He assured him that they were trying to get help as soon as they could. Clifford's reply came very plainly, "Daddy, I want to be a Christian."

Nathan told him, "You are forgiven by us. Just ask God to forgive you and He will hear." With the noise of the car and everything, they couldn't hear his prayer but thought they heard "Father" and "Forgive". He was also saying other things but they could not make out what they were.

Soon after this, Clifford asked Kevin to come back and hold him. Kevin crawled over the seat to grant his request. Nathan and Kevin began to feel that they had better get an ambulance or next thing they wouldn't even make it to the hospital. Nathan quickly drove to the medic station. When Kevin told Clifford where they were, he could tell he relaxed somewhat. We think he felt help was near. But no one was at the station, and even the phones were dead. When Clifford heard no one was around, Kevin felt him stiffen again. As Nathan was trying to think where to go next, Kevin thought of the Sheetz gas station in town. They raced there and called 911.

As they were sitting there waiting, the rescue squad came. Clifford wondered why they came. Kevin told him, "The ambulance isn't here yet, and that's what they're waiting for."

"They will have to come soon!" was Clifford's urgent reply. They waited around five minutes until the ambulance arrived. Kevin said when he told Clifford the ambulance was there, he once again relaxed and even his breathing became more normal.

The paramedics got Clifford into the ambulance but didn't want Kevin or Nathan to ride along. They told Nathan they were not sure which hospital they would be going to because they were both full. Nathan told them he would prefer Chambersburg since that is the hospital we use. They finally decided to go to Chambersburg but told Nathan not to try to keep up with them.

Nathan called me once the ambulance got there and told me Clifford had given his heart to the Lord. I hardly know how to write how I felt when I heard that. I just felt everything will be all right. Yet I knew he was very sick. I also was somewhat relieved because I thought he was finally with those who could help him.

Nathan and Kevin then started driving toward Chambersburg, but decided Kevin could go to work since it was about 3:30 a.m. Nathan dropped Kevin off at work and went on to the hospital. When he arrived he saw he was ahead of the ambulance.

The hospital personnel were waiting for Nathan because I had called them from home. So Nathan went ahead and registered Clifford and gave the symptoms of what he knew. By that time the ambulance had arrived. Nathan had to go to another room off of the emergency room. There was no time wasted. At least six personnel were working on Clifford. They constantly informed Nathan as to what they were doing and how things were going — but they soon told Nathan they were not able to get Clifford stabilized. At this point Nathan called me to let me know the sad news.

I decided right away I'm going in. I quickly called my sister, Joanne, and both our parents, letting them know things don't look good and asked for prayer. Grandma Ebersole said she could come over and Joanne said either she or Laura would come. Julene and I left after I got the rest of the family up to chore. Oh, how it tore at my heart to think dear Clifford was so near to slipping away and I wasn't with him.

Almost as soon as we got to the hospital around 4:00, a nurse came in and said, "I am so sorry but we are almost finished!" She said his heart had stopped once and they got it going again. He was bleeding internally and they couldn't get his blood to clot. While she was still in with us, the doctor came in and gently, sadly broke the news. "We are done. He is gone." What a comfort to know he was with the Lord where pain and sickness would not touch him again. It was also a comfort to have our minister and his wife (my sister), our older deacon and his wife, and our young deacon come in at this time.

The doctor told us they will clean him up a bit then we could come look at him. Nathan, Julene, and I went to see Clifford first and then the rest came. We then gathered in the other room again and shared some comforting thoughts from the Word — the only place to find true comfort and rest at a time like this!

Once the coroner got there he informed us they will need

to do an autopsy because of his age. He said they will have to send his body to Allentown since that is where it will be done. The doctor told us there was a massive infection going on that caused the bleeding, and the bleeding is what finally took Clifford's life. He said they will let us know as soon as they get the culture results because the rest of us may need to take medication. Also they needed the cultures for the safety of those working on Clifford. They said it will probably be twenty-four hours until the results come back, because that is how long it usually takes a culture to grow.

At this point we decided to leave the hospital. The ministry took care of our one vehicle and we went home together. It was hard to leave without Clifford and to realize this was the beginning of going on without him.

We had decided to meet to make funeral arrangements at 10:00 a.m. Around 2:00 p.m. they called and said that the cultures had already grown enough to give the results. Clifford had Neisseria meningitidis which is a bacterial meningitis. This caused the breaking of his blood vessels in the last stages of the sickness, and finally took his life. In most cases of this they have twenty-four to seventy-two hours until all the symptoms show up. In Clifford's case, from the first that we knew he didn't feel well till he passed away, was only sixteen hours.

We do not want to question God's workings. But it was comforting to hear the hospital staff, and later the paramedics, say we did all we could. One of them told us she knew cases where they lost limbs or vital organs. So once again we were so thankful that Clifford would never have pain or another operation again. *"The Lord hath given and the Lord hath taken away, blessed be the name of the Lord."*

One Month Later

February 16, 2001 was a special day because the school children were home for teachers' visitation. We had been remodeling some of the rooms in our house, so Leslie finished up the closets in the middle room that day. The younger boys, Chris and Stanley, were working on the culti-packer.

Michael had some homework at the beginning of the day. He wanted so bad to work on his cousin Duane's scrapbook page. Duane was very sick and could not come to Clifford's funeral. So I told Michael to hurry up with his homework, then he can work on the page. That certainly helped him get done! He was done in record time. He got right down to working on his page for Duane.

Then I suggested that Michael read to the little girls a while. That was something Michael usually enjoyed and the girls loved it. He was very good with the girls and was a great help in keeping them entertained.

Everyone was here for dinner except Kevin who had a regular work day. After dinner I told Chris, Stanley, and Michael they should take the bunk beds apart that Leslie and Clifford had slept in and take them over to the room the boys were sleeping in now. Leslie was not ready to sleep in that room. The memories of Clifford were too real yet.

We still had some mattresses on the floor from overnight company since Clifford's funeral. So the boys were very excited about having a nice bedroom, and a bunk bed for each boy. They had lots of fun taking them apart and putting them back together. It looked so nice when they were finished and the beds were made. It was extra special to Michael because it would be the first night he would sleep in this bunk bed.

When they were finished, Nathan, Chris, and Stanley went back to work at taking the culti-packer apart. After Michael fed the chickens he stayed outside and helped the rest. It was a bit surprising that he stayed out because it was rainy, damp, and cold, and he liked it inside most of the time.

At 4:00 Michael came in and laid down on the sofa saying his head hurt. Right away I thought about Clifford, so I took his temperature but he had no fever. I relaxed a little and thought, *"He is probably getting one of his bad headaches again."* He had such bad headaches sometimes that he'd throw up. I got him some Tylenol but he didn't like taking pills, so I worked with him a bit until he was ready to take it. He was crying some so I asked if he would drink hot tea if I made him some. He thought he would.

I made him some tea and he did drink it but I saw he was very uncomfortable and still crying at times. I asked if his head still hurts. He said, "No, it doesn't hurt anymore but my knee hurts so bad!" I hardly knew what to think of his knee hurting, or what to do about it.

The family came in for supper but Michael did not want to eat. So once again the family gathered for a supper without one family member. It seemed like a big hole because it was just a month that Clifford had left our family circle.

Michael was restless and pulled the cover up over his face because he didn't like the light in his eyes. He would stretch his leg out then pull it up — stretch it and pull it up — again and again, because it hurt him so. Like as for any of the children, it hurt me to see him in pain but I couldn't do much to relieve him. We left him lie on the sofa while we had devotions. In our prayers we asked the Lord to help make Michael feel better. After devotions we all sat there trying to decide why Michael's knee hurts so bad, and what to do so he might feel better.

I remembered when Kevin was younger he used to cry because his legs hurt sometimes. And we noticed it was especially bad when it was damp and rainy. So I thought maybe that was what Michael's problem was. Kevin remembered that too, and said how bad it used to hurt but after he would go to sleep it would be okay and he would sleep all night. I did look at his knee a couple of times but nothing showed.

At 9:00 p.m. we decided to go to bed. When Michael got up and walked he really limped and cried in pain. Oh, how I pitied him! I took his temperature again. It showed normal but I thought he should take Tylenol for his hurting knee so he could sleep. Just before he went upstairs he had to throw up. I thought it was probably because of all the pain, or maybe from his headache. Nathan told me later he had wondered, after Michael threw up, if we should take him to the hospital. But with the fact that he had no fever he thought he should be okay. The state nurse had told us an elevated fever was one of the more sure signs of meningitis. At that time, I did not have fears of Michael having what Clifford had. If that would have been in my mind at all, I could not have gone to bed and slept. I did pray that God would care for our dear Michael. Finally, everyone went to sleep.

Nathan woke up at 2:00 a.m. and heard someone use the bathroom. He thought of Michael, so went over to check on him. He was the one who had just been in the bathroom. Nathan asked him if he was sick. He shook his head and said, "No." Then Nathan asked if he threw up, and again he said, "No." He said he just went to the bathroom. So Nathan checked things out in the bathroom and everything look okay. He went over to Michael and here he was already sleeping! Nathan felt his head for a fever and it felt normal. He came back to bed. I knew he had checked on him so I was content with that, and we both went back to sleep.

At 2:45, Leslie knocked on our bedroom door and said Michael was throwing up. I was awake in no time and right then I did think about Clifford and what he had. I *ran* over to Michael! He was throwing up when I got there. I quickly pulled the cover back and looked at his knee. To my fear, his knee was black and blue around a very large area. I was beginning to feel very weak. I pulled his night clothes up and there were black and blue blotches all over him. I wanted to just cry out and collapse but I ran over to Nathan and said, "It is the same as Clifford had! What shall we do?!!"

My mouth went so dry I could hardly talk, and I felt so very weak. Together we hurried just as fast as we could. I went over and helped Michael get ready to go to the hospital. Nathan came right downstairs and called the hospital, telling them we are coming right in with a son with the same symptoms of our son who had died a month ago in their hospital. He told them we were not waiting for an ambulance but were coming in as fast as possible.

Michael walked over to the steps and Nathan carried him down. He stood at the table and I wrapped an afghan around him. Nathan carried him out and I sat in the back seat with him. It was now 3:05 a.m.

At this time we had high hopes of getting help for our dear son. He did not seem near as sick as Clifford and he was very calm. The children at home also felt we'd be able to get help.

They were very concerned when we woke them up. Kevin, Julene, and Leslie hurried around almost frantically, trying to get us off as soon as possible. They did all they could to help and assured us they'd take care of the chores.

Soon after we left, Julene asked Kevin if they should call the deacon and let him know, and maybe put it on the hotline for prayer. He didn't know about that, but finally decided to call and let them decide what to do. There was almost a constant prayer on their hearts.

The house looked like we had come to the end of the week and it was high time to clean. Julene decided she must start even though she didn't feel like doing anything. She thought that Michael would probably be in the hospital for a while and there would be people seeing the house, so the three of them worked together. Julene didn't want to think that we'd need to gather to plan another funeral but the thought wouldn't leave.

Before they got very far with the cleaning, our minister (my sister's husband), called and wanted to know more details. Julene told him that Michael already had spots over him, and yet he didn't seem as sick as Clifford had been. He encouraged them that they'd probably be able to get help this time. Then my sister got on the phone and offered to help wherever they might need it. That was very much appreciated, although at that point they felt they would be fine.

Meanwhile, we were speeding to the hospital with a constant prayer on our minds with very few words. We hadn't gone far when I asked Michael if he knows where we are going. He nodded his head and said, "To the hospital."

He was lying on the back seat and I was sitting at his head. We had gone a bit farther when he got restless and acted as though he wanted to sit up. I remembered that Nathan thought the more Clifford moved around, the worse his breathing became, so I told Michael, "Just stay laying — it might be better." I also started rubbing his head. He laid down again — it seemed to be taking so long to get to the hospital. But I saw Nathan had the four-ways on and was going *fast.*

Then Michael got very restless, lifted his head and said something but I did not understand, so I asked, "What, Michael?" And again, he said the same thing. Again, I did not understand. It was so hard on me because he tried four or five times, and each time it was exactly the same thing but I just could not understand it! It was not that he said it too quiet, it just was not plain. I had my hand where I could feel the pulse at his neck. After I said, "Michael, Mama is here and we are going for help as fast as we can," he laid down again. I thought I didn't feel his pulse anymore but quickly decided maybe I just was not feeling at the right spot anymore. In my anguish, I urged Nathan, "Drive *fast!* I'm not sure we are going to make it!" I saw Michael's color change and I called his name. I tried to talk to him but he did not respond and his eyes did not move at all. I wanted to push the thought far from my mind that Michael might have gone to meet Clifford and the Lord.

When we arrived at the hospital, Nathan quickly carried Michael in but he told them he thinks he might be gone. There were people all around immediately. As the hospital staff took over we had to go off to the side room where we were just one month ago. As we walked back, Nathan saw a man that must have been in a fight. His face was all cut up. When Nathan told me, I had to think how wicked this world was. It helped us to think that our boys are safe!

The same nurse that told us the sad news of Clifford, came in and told us there was little hope for Michael. His heart had stopped, but with the machine it was going again.

They would probably soon stop it. They told us he had a fever of 105 degrees. The "why's" were going through our minds so fast. This was *not* to happen! We were treated with antibiotics. *Where did Michael pick this up? Why was it just his knee that hurt, and no fever?* It seemed nothing made sense — we were up against — there was only one source to turn to, and that was the Lord. He would be the help that was needed from here away.

Meanwhile, our children at home were nurturing their hopes. They figured we were probably waiting to call till we were sure Michael was stabilized. When the phone finally rang, Leslie and Julene waited breathlessly while Kevin answered. When they could tell Nathan and Kevin were discussing chores, they thought everything must be fine. Then Kevin asked, "How is he?" They saw a terrible look come over Kevin's face, he let out a groan, laid his head on his arms, and cried. They thought it couldn't be! Not again! But it was true. How our hearts ached for our dear ones at home. How we longed to be there to comfort them! They waited in anguish till we came home.

Our deacon and his wife came to the hospital. We told them he was gone. It was helpful when we saw how hard it was on them too. Already there were others standing by us. Our minister and his wife (my sister) came too. Again the sad news was told and we could tell their hearts bled for us. Our younger deacon and his wife also came and we felt the same about them. Words failed us. We just said, "We don't know what to say."

We went to look at Michael one last time before we left without him. I thought, *"Oh, how small he looks!"* He had that same dark color as Clifford had over his skin with black and blue blotches everywhere across his body. They told us the black and blue marks were from his blood vessels breaking. Although Michael did not have the internal bleeding Clifford had, he bled to death because of the massive infection. The bleeding was the last stage of the disease.

As we traveled homeward, it seemed we were numbed. This just didn't seem true — that Michael had now left our family circle too.

There were many people that came to help. Already we could feel our brotherhood was hurting too and would not let us down, but would do what they could.

When the state nurse came, we told her that we have lots of questions. With tears running down her cheeks, she said, "I wish we had answers, but we don't!" She said that this had never happened before, that the family being treated had another family member getting it. She agreed that the Lord's ways are above our ways.

Friday, after Michael's funeral, the school and church people were all treated with antibiotics. Then one-and-one-half weeks later we were all vaccinated with a vaccine that was to be good for three years.

We do have fears that we've never had before. We have prayed for help to look at sickness in our children with simple common sense. Depending on how we are feeling, we could lose our common sense in how serious the sickness is that we have at the moment.

We had been keenly feeling the empty spot that Clifford left. It seemed we should see him just anytime, because it was long enough that he was gone... We do wonder *why? Why? Why?!* But we know God does what is best and He does control all things. One real blessing is, we know our dear sons are safe and no one can pluck them from the Father's hands.

We have felt, in a very real way, the prayers of the

brotherhood, family, and friends. We are so thankful for all the prayers, cards, and help given us over those times.

We know and feel the Lord is good. These experiences help us long to be faithful so that some day we can be with our Lord, and dear Clifford and Michael.

May we pray for each other and not faint by the way.

—Nathan & Julia Ebersole
Shippensburg, Pennsylvania

In Memory of Clifford and Michael Ebersole

The hand of God has touched our midst
And called a soul to Heaven
He cried unto his Savior dear
And his sins were all forgiven.

Clifford tried to be content
With pain and scars he bore,
Now in the Father's tender care,
They are known and felt no more.

Sixteen years, so young he left us,
Nevermore him here we'll see
Now with Christ our loving Father
He's from sin and sorrow free.

One month later, how can it be,
Death's angel again so loud did call,
Now Michael too, has left us,
God has a purpose for this all.

Ten short years to him were granted,
Happy, innocent, and free,
And he now for us is waiting
Far beyond the crystal sea.

Father, Mother, sisters, brothers,
Do no longer for us grieve,
May the happy days of yore
In your hearts fond mem'ries leave.

Schoolmates, teachers, friends, and loved ones,
Will you join us too, someday?
Make Christ the Lord your Savior now
Humbly bow to Him and pray.

Someone will be the next to follow,
Perhaps that someone will be you,
Have you surrendered all to Jesus,
Are you faithful, loyal, and true?

So dear loved ones who are grieving
May we all in Heaven meet,
When the toils of life are over,
Will the circle be complete?

—Poet Unknown

Kevin Roy Lehman

February 5, 1989 to April 22, 2002 (13 years)

Here One Moment — Gone The Next

Thelma Lehman, Mother

It was a busy Monday, as usual. I had gotten up early that day and started making a special meal to take to a family from church that had just had a new baby. I had also started the other Monday chores, and had taken Kevin to school. On our way to pick up other children, Kevin talked about whether he wants to continue in school after the next year, or do his work at home for grades 9-12 as his sister Doris did. He said that he would like to go to school because he would enjoy taking shop classes, but was undecided. Little did we know that he would not have to make that decision.

In the afternoon the other driver brought Kevin home. He was in the house for about fifteen minutes when I asked him to go get the mail. I didn't realize that would be the last time that I would talk to him. He hopped on the go-cart and went out the lane with the dog running along. I am glad that we were not watching. I hadn't thought about it that he didn't return until Doris looked out the window and asked what the pickup truck was doing in the field. I went to the window to see and thought of Kevin. I ran outside and yelled for him. He didn't answer so I took the car and hurried out to the road. There was the dog, hurting. He couldn't walk, (and it took him a long time to get better.)

Where was Kevin? I didn't see him or the go-cart right away, but then realized that he must be under the pickup. I stooped down to look. There he was, so still. He was in front of the back wheel on the driver's side of the truck, but still partially on the go-cart. I talked to him and touched him with no response. I was sure that he was gone. By this time I saw Doris was outside the house. I yelled to her to call 911 and bring the cell phone.

When she came out I called my husband, Sidney, who was a truck driver. I told him that I thought Kevin was gone. He said that he would be home as soon as possible. He was in Ohio, about seven hours away. Later, I talked to his boss and he said if Sidney calls home again I should not tell him that Kevin did actually pass away (for Sidney's safety). The boss said he would go to meet him, and tell him the sad news, then bring the truck home. Sidney got home about 10:30 p.m. It seemed like a long time...

When I got to the scene, the pickup truck door was standing wide open and the driver was not around. Later I found out that the driver ran to the closest house for help. Neighbors came to the scene, also, a church friend who was on the ambulance crew but not on duty at the time. He was close by and had heard the ambulance call. He confirmed that Kevin was gone. He had checked for a pulse several times, but couldn't find any. He felt that Kevin had died instantly from a broken neck.

It wasn't long until the ambulance came. I'm glad that I got to the scene before the ambulance did because they would not have let me see Kevin. Doris and I were asked to sit in the ambulance.

Our son, Jeff, and our two daughters, Carol and Brenda, were notified at work and were soon there too. Family, friends and ambulance personnel sat with us until the coroner came and they removed Kevin from under the pickup. A neighbor man had taken our car to the house, and also gathered our mail from the field. The ambulance drove us up the lane to our house.

A few families in the area that had recently had their children die suddenly, came to give us support, also church friends and family. Many of them sat with us until Sidney came home. It was so hard to believe that Kevin was no longer here. (One time that first evening I thought I saw Kevin sitting there with us.) Our minister and his wife stayed until they thought we should try to get some rest.

We didn't sleep much that night, or that whole week. We would toss and turn and finally fall asleep. In the morning we would wake up early and Kevin's death was the first thing we thought of. The next few days were busy — meeting with the undertaker, planning the funeral, picking a grave site, etc.

The funeral was on Friday — a tiring day of much grief. Our minister preached a wonderful, comforting message of seeing Kevin again in heaven. Family, friends, and school children were there to bring us comfort and support. Grades 7-12 sang at the grave side. The one song that they sang was "The Music of Heaven" — one of Kevin's favorites.

There were many adjustments to be made. I no longer had to drive school children as he was our youngest child. Someone had to do the chores that he was responsible for. Life at school was difficult, and different too, for the students and teachers. They took a collection and bought a flowering crab apple tree for us. The seven seventh grade boys came and planted it in our yard. We planted flowers around the tree with a plaque in memory of Kevin that reads:

No Farewell Words Were Spoken,
No Time To Say Goodbye,
You Were Gone Before We Knew It,
And Only God Knows Why.

We are so thankful that he had accepted the Lord as his Savior. About a year earlier he had come to me before school one morning and said that he would like to become a Christian. I prayed with him and helped him to find peace. We were rejoicing! He and Doris had just finished instruction class and on Thursday we were going to have a meeting to plan their baptism for the near future, but plans were changed. We had a viewing for Kevin instead. From time to time he had asked questions about how this or that was in heaven, and we would just tell him that we would have to wait and see. We never thought that he would be the first one of our family to find out.

Kevin liked to work on engines and had a dream of building an engine that ran on alcohol. Kevin had just talked to one of his friends from church Sunday evening (the evening before he died). They had planned to work on this project together but never talked more than just a few words together on the phone before. This time they talked at least twenty minutes. They did not realize that this would be the last time that they would talk. He had asked me a few days earlier if he could plant corn in the garden. He also asked me that morning if I had any yeast. I found the calculator beside his bed. He was trying to figure out how much yeast he would need to make alcohol. Later we found out that he had asked his science teacher about it also. He was very active and always trying to figure things out.

Where would we be without God in our lives? How would we go on without Jesus, the great Comforter by our sides? How would it be without the many friends and family that have helped us so much in times like these? We realize that God could have prevented this from happening but we also know that God makes no mistakes and all things are under His control. Sometimes we just wonder "why"? We accept it as His will because He is there to help us through each day.

It helps a lot to talk and to share with others that have had the same experiences. There are quite a few families in our area that recently had sudden deaths of their children. It also helped me to make a scrapbook, which I'm still working at. HIS MEMORY LIVES ON IN OUR HEARTS!

The following was written by one of Kevin's school friends.

Kevin Roy was liked by all he met,
Eager to learn new things everywhere he went,
Very talented, he loved to sing
In many hearts some happiness to bring -
Now he's singing praises to the King

Riding in the go-cart out the lane
Obediently he went to get the mail
Yet he didn't see the truck until too late

Little did he know he soon will die
Even though he loved the Lord on high
Heaven welcomed him with so much joy
Many here will grieve for this dear boy
All of us with Jesus in our hearts
Never will in heaven have to part
Missed by all who knew him

~

School Memories of Kevin Roy Lehman

Anita F. Weaver, Teacher

On Sunday evening, April 21, 2002, I was visiting with several friends, some of whom were teachers also. As teachers do, we were discussing the many aspects of our calling. Somehow the fact that I enjoy the challenge of adolescents in seventh and eighth grades entered the conversation. One of my friends asked me, "Why?"

I thought briefly and replied, "Let me tell you about Kevin Roy Lehman."

At our school in seventh grade the students come downstairs to high school. To go from an ordinary classroom to a class by class schedule is quite a change, often traumatic.

Kevin Roy brought a massive amount of energy with him, and he tested the bounds of the system in every direction. He asked questions all the time. His questions were difficult to answer because we seldom knew when he was sincere and when it was an effort to sidetrack the class. The first quarter was rough. Kevin Roy is interesting to talk to and funny to watch so even when he was deliberately disruptive, the others were entertained. Finally, after several events, and following discussions with the administrator, Kevin Roy chose the better way.

The change is inspiring. His energy never flags. He still bounces into class and chatters right up until the last bell. He still asks a multitude of questions. He still entertains the others. But there the similarities end.

His questions now have a definite purpose; he wants to learn. He obeys promptly even when I just frown in disapproval. His energy is still phenomenal, but he never aims to deliberately cause havoc. He has become a student that is fun to teach.

On April 22, 2002, when I answered Kevin Roy's questions in the library, I did not think of the discussion of the previous evening. When he grinned at me as he raced from the classroom at 3:00 p.m. I still did not think of it.

It was after the shocking phone call around 4:00 p.m., only after the initial shock wore off, that I remembered. The questions I will no longer answer, the running footsteps that will no longer sound, the grin I will no longer see — these losses are balanced by the memory of a boy who was willing to change, willing to be what God wanted him to be.

—Anita F. Weaver, Teacher

—Sidney & Thelma Lehman
Bethel, Pennsylvania

Brian Lynn Stutzman

October 16, 1986 to December 13, 2002 (16 years)

Precious Memories

Barb Stutzman, Mother

Around November 25, 2002, Brian (16) started complaining that he has a backache. We took him for chiropractor treatments twice that week. I can still hear him say, after the first treatment, how good he felt. Then in a day or so, he was in pain again and could hardly lift his arm. The next week he had trouble breathing and began coughing.

December 3, I took Brian to the doctor. The doctor said he had bronchitis, also the possibility of a pinched nerve in his back. He prescribed pain pills and something for bronchitis.

Thursday, December 5, Brian was a lot worse, so back to the doctor we went. This time he gave him a shot for bronchitis. When we came home from the doctor around noon, Brian decided he felt good enough to go to work.

He worked for his uncle at a woodworking shop, and really enjoyed it.

Friday, December 6, Brian went to work again. (Little did we realize that this would be his last day of work on this earth.)

Monday morning when he came downstairs, he was coughing, wheezing, and breathing hard. My husband, Gary, said he should go back to bed because he won't be able to go to work. Brian went back to bed until about 9:00 a.m., then we took him to the doctor again. This time the doctor took a chest x-ray. The x-ray didn't look normal, so the doctor told us to go to the hospital the next day for a cat scan.

We scheduled Gary's aunt to take us to the hospital the next day. When it was time to go, I went upstairs to help Brian get ready. He said he didn't know what was wrong — he just didn't have any energy. Finally, I got him down the stairs. (He told me later that he had to talk to himself so he wouldn't panic.) He was so sick by then that we took him to the emergency room. We got there around 9:30 a.m. and by 11:00 they told us they were quite sure he had a type of lymphoma cancer. What a shock! More tests and cat scans were done. We were told the type of cancer Brian had was lymphoblastoma — a very fast-growing cancer. The doctor talked about starting chemotherapy that afternoon yet, but then for some reason they didn't after all.

They gave us a room with two beds, and I spent the night at the hospital with Brian. He couldn't sleep so we talked most of the night — something I will always treasure as long as I live. I asked him if he realized that this could be very serious. He said, "Yes, Mom. But..." and shrugged his shoulders. He was so calm and patient about everything. I said, "Brian, pray a lot." He replied, "I am going to." And I think he did.

Wednesday, December 11, around 11:00 a.m., they took

him to surgery to put in a port for the chemotherapy. The doctors told me it was to be a simple procedure and they wouldn't need to put him to sleep. He would be in surgery until noon. Well, 12:00 came and went and there was still no word from Brian. I was getting a little nervous, but asked the Lord to help me.

It wasn't long till a nurse came, walking at a fast pace. She said, "Mrs. Stutzman, we've run into problems. There is a doctor out in the hall that wants to talk to you."

The doctor said they had put in the port. Brian talked to them as he crawled from the operating table to his bed. When he got onto his bed, he panicked, and everything stopped. They were now giving him CPR. The doctor needed my consent to put the heart-lung machine on him. He said he could have him open and the machine on in two minutes, with my okay. He said without it there is no chance that Brian would survive.

I was in shock, started shaking uncontrollably, and said they should go ahead. I couldn't understand where Gary was. He had been planning on being there with me. Here I found out he was on the sixth floor waiting for Brian to come back to his room. The nurses just kept telling him to wait there as Brian should be back any minute.

Finally, three nurses went to find Gary for me. They found him, along with my sister, sister-in-law, and our three other children. When the family saw those nurses, they knew something was wrong.

Once we were all together, they updated us on Brian's condition. They told us his heart was beating on its own and his other organs were all working, except he wasn't breathing on his own. He was on a ventilator. Gary asked the doctor how long Brian was without oxygen. He just said it was a long time. We later found out it was close to twenty minutes which was too long, but they wouldn't tell us that at the time so we wouldn't give up. They then told us they will take him to Intensive Care where we could see him after a while.

We were not prepared to see him lying on the bed so lifeless, and with a tracheotomy. We felt Brian could hear us as that evening before our daughter, Lorinda, went home, she went back into his room and told him she was going home. She said she would come back the next day— and he shed tears. Later, Gary asked him some questions and he shed more tears. A couple of times we asked him to squeeze our hands, but he never did.

About noon Thursday, they told us he was going backwards. Gary and I went to his room. Gary said, "Brian, I hope we can all be with you some day." Another tear flowed from the corner of his eye and his lips quivered. We will always wonder whether he wanted to tell us something, but couldn't.

Friday morning, the doctor told us they wanted to take brain scans to make sure there was no activity. Then with our consent, they would take the ventilator off that afternoon. Three brain tests were done, but there was no activity in his brain anymore. So we called some friends and relatives and told them if they wanted to see Brian, they needed to come to the hospital soon. One nurse estimated there were close to one hundred people there when they took the ventilator off.

Brian passed away peacefully at 4:20 Friday afternoon, December 13, 2002.

We surely do miss him, but wouldn't want to wish him back into this sinful world.

—Gary and Barb Stutzman
Nappanee, Indiana

Chadwin Todd Reinford

May 22, 1999 to March 22, 2001 (22 months)

In God's Hands

Lois Reinford, Mother

Wednesday evening, March 21, 2001, Tim came home from work and asked me what I would think of him staying home from work the next day and going to a sale. We talked it over, and really never made a decision as we needed to get ready to go to parent-teachers' meeting that evening. We got ready and left for our scheduled time to talk to the children's school teacher. We took Chad with us and left the other four children at home with Martha Klippenstein who was boarding at our place. The rest came later when it was time for the evening church service to begin.

The next morning, March 22, Tim had decided that he would stay home from work and go to the sale. He also planned to grind feed for the steers as that was a job that was hard to get at sometimes when he was gone all day.

Then he thought that he would still have time in the late afternoon to kill a steer that we wanted to cut up and put into the freezer on Saturday. This was only Thursday, so I agreed that would be a good idea.

Tim left around 10:00 a.m. for the sale taking five-year-old Carla and three-year-old Gregory with him.

I had started potty-training Chad two days before this, so I thought this was a good opportunity to work with him without any interruptions from the other preschoolers. I also did some sewing and washed clothes that day.

Chad seemed to miss his brothers and sisters and hardly knew what to do with himself. For some reason he was a little fussy, and acted tired enough that I decided to put him to bed for an earlier-than-usual nap. I rocked him and he soon fell asleep. I very seldom rocked him to sleep anymore, but I'll always be glad that I did that day. He was asleep by 10:30 and slept until 1:15.

I went upstairs to get him out of his crib. It seemed his first thoughts were as to where the other children were. As we were coming down the stairs, he said, "Where's Harley?" I said, "Harlan and Luanne are at school. Carla and Greg went with Dad, and *you* are Mom's little boy today!" (Harlan was eight years old and Luanne was six.) He smiled one of his radiant smiles that were so common, and gave me a big hug while patting my back with his chubby little hand. Little did I realize that would be the last time he would pat my back.

I heated up some dinner for him, and he ate happily.

When he was done eating, he started playing with his tractor in the living room. It wasn't long until I noticed that he had messed himself, so I prepared to give him a bath. He always loved bath time. As I started running the water, he said, "Mom, dump." That was his way of telling me to be sure and put bubble bath into his water. I washed him and then let him play with bath toys a while.

Martha was working for someone else, but was planning to bring the school children home. It was soon time for them to come, so I told Chad that Harlan and Luanne would soon be home. He immediately said, "I want out," and tried to climb out of the tub. So I got him out and dressed him. By that time the children were at home. Chad was so glad to see them!

Tim and the other two children came home shortly after that. Chad was begging, "I wanna' go out." He loved to go outside, and now that the others were home, that was where he wanted to be.

It might have been close to one-half hour until Tim went out again, and Chad didn't go out until then. Tim helped him get ready, putting on his coat, boots and mittens.

Tim ground feed before he went to the sale but needed to put some supplements in the mixer yet before he unloaded it in the barn. While he was doing that, the children played. Chad rode his little car on the cement pad in front of the garage door. At one point, I looked out and saw him there. That is the last time I saw him alive.

Before Tim was done unloading feed, Norm (his brother) called to see whether Tim had gotten anything for him at the sale. He was planning to head for town and wanted to pick his things up if Tim had gotten what he wanted. So Tim came in to call him back to tell him that he had gotten some things for him.

As Tim was leaving the house again, I noticed all the vehicles outside. Stephen Leinbach, who was also boarding here, had just come home. His pickup was still running as he was planning to leave soon again. The tractor was running and Tim's pickup and trailer were not parked in the shed where they usually were. So I said to Tim, "Be careful and watch the children. Especially watch our little Chaddy boy." Tim said, "I will," and walked out the door. *Tim was always careful with the children. I trusted them into his care completely when they were with him.*

Tim was soon done unloading feed and backed into the shed to unhook the grinder-mixer. Next, he planned to take the tractor to the back part of the barn where he would kill the steer. For some reason he wondered if he should really kill the steer yet that day, or wait until another time, but decided to go ahead. Chad was in the shed while he unhooked the mixer and wanted to ride on the bucket, so Tim put him in. This was something that he seldom allowed the children to do, but that day for some reason he didn't really give it a second thought. He wasn't going far — just back behind the barn.

The other children were in the barn feeding the smaller steers since Tim had just finished grinding feed for them. When they saw that Chad was getting a ride, they all came running except Carla who continued to feed the animals. So Tim stopped to let them on. He had just started going again and was turning to head into the pasture. As he turned, Chad fell off the bucket. Luanne saw him fall and yelled, but before it registered in Tim's mind why she yelled, he felt a bump. Looking down, he saw Chad lying on the ground.

As soon as he saw him he knew he was gone. Chad never moved after he was run over. We were thankful we didn't have to watch him suffer. But oh, it was so sudden! We couldn't fully comprehend it at the time.

This happened around 4:30 p.m. Chad was riding on the left side of the bucket when he fell off, and because Tim was turning, he was driven over by the right front tire.

Tim does not remember stopping the tractor, but he had stopped with Chad lying between the front and back tires. The first I knew anything happened was when Tim came to the front door of the house to tell me to come quickly, that he had run over Chad! He had a terrible look on his face! As Tim was telling me to come, I heard the rest of the children screaming and crying in horror.

I quickly went out with Tim and walked over to where Chad lay. He was bleeding badly and it was very obvious that life had fled. He lay so still! There are no words to explain all the thoughts and emotions that we experienced in those few moments.

Harlan ran to the barn to tell Carla, and she came running. So all the children saw the terrible sight that would haunt them for days to come.

We tried to decide what to do next. There was no question whether there was any life left in Chad. The other children needed us right now.

Tim had told Martha to call Norms right away. She made that phone call while I went out with Tim. She was still talking when we came back in. Tim had just thought about it that Norm was probably already on his way to town, so he took the phone from Martha and talked to Phyllis a little. She said she would call his cellular phone right away.

We held the children and tried to calm them. Greg, especially, was very upset and kept saying, "I'm scared! I'm scared!" And, "I want to play with Chad some more!"

We decided to bring Chad into the house. It just didn't seem right to let him outside. So Tim went out and carried him in. We laid him on a sheet on the counter and covered his head with the sheet. Everything seemed so unreal. We wished we could wake up and find it all a bad dream. I remember thinking that this just *can't* be happening to us!

It always happened to someone else. But another look at the still form lying there made it all too real.

Norm arrived after several minutes. But because Tim took the phone before Martha was done talking to Phyllis, Norm did not know until he got here whether Chad was still alive or not. We felt bad about that.

We all gathered in the living room and prayed. Then Norm thought it would be best to call 911.

We soon heard sirens and it wasn't long until our lane was full of emergency vehicles. The first men to arrive ran into the house and straight to Chad. One of them listened for a heartbeat, then made a motion to Norm that he was gone. The police came in and questioned Tim. They were perplexed at why we had waited to call 911, so Tim tried to explain. When he questioned Norm, he wondered why we called him first before calling 911, since he was only a brother. Norm told him that he is also our pastor. That seemed to satisfy him.

I'm not sure why we didn't call 911 right away, except that we knew there was no hope anyway. And being in shock, we just didn't think that far. We were thankful later that it didn't create any problems, although the police questioned both Tim and Norm real good.

Our deacon, Kenneth Witmer, arrived while the ambulance and police were still here. After people cleared out a bit, we all gathered in the living room and had a time of prayer again. Kenneth read some comforting scriptures. He also made phone calls, letting the rest of the church people know about the accident.

After a while, the coroner came to pronounce Chad dead. I felt sorry for Tim with all the commotion of people coming and going, and all the questions he had to answer while I could stay in the background away from it all.

Sometime during all the commotion Phyllis Reinford had arrived. I was glad for her help with the children. They were much calmer by then, but still wanted to be held. Harvey and Marilyn Witmer, our bishop and his wife, arrived after Phyllis, and Anna Witmer (Kenneth's wife) came soon after that. We were so grateful for their presence.

While we were waiting for the undertaker to come, we all gathered in the living room for another time of prayer. More tears were shed and comforting words were spoken. It meant so much to us to have our ministry come so soon to share with us.

The undertaker came around 7:30 p.m. and talked a few things over, then gave us time alone before he took the body. We all gathered around in the dining room and kitchen. Harvey read some scriptures, then Norm lead in prayer. The undertaker was then called in. He soon left, taking the body of our little boy with him.

The ministry then left one by one. Several families from church stopped in yet that night. It meant so much to know that others cared. One thing that meant a lot to us was that Dennis Hoover came and did our chores that evening. He came back the next four evenings to do chores. Stephen took care of the chores in the mornings.

Sleep did not come easy for any of us that night. Carla and Greg had missed their naps that day since they had gone with Tim to the sale. That turned out to be a blessing. Once they fell asleep, they slept good.

Harlan fell asleep downstairs so Tim carried him up to his bed, but he awoke again. Luanne finally settled down, too. Then Harlan came to our room and said he couldn't sleep. So we read some Bible verses to him and prayed with him, and he soon went to sleep. Luanne woke up during the night crying, but it didn't take long to get her back to sleep again.

As for Tim and I, we didn't get much sleep that night. We were up early Friday morning. None of us had eaten supper the evening before, except for Greg. So we knew we should eat breakfast, even though we didn't feel like it. It was hard to sit down at the table without Chad. How we missed his usual "Good morning" and his happy, smiling self as we ate a small breakfast.

There were many decisions and plans to be made in the next several days. We never realized before how much there is to decide in preparation for a funeral, and how hard it is to make those decisions when the mind is numb.

Friday was an especially hard day. There were so many things to remind us of Chad! We met at the church that morning to make funeral plans with the ministry. We were in the van ready to leave for the church when Tim opened the garage door, and looking in his mirror to back out, he saw Chad's little car that he had been riding only minutes before the accident. Tim could hardly bring himself to get out of the van to move it.

After making the funeral plans we, along with Norm and Kenneth, went to the funeral home to pick out a casket, order memorial folders, etc. It was the first funeral for our church, and the undertaker was not familiar with our procedures. He had lots of questions and we were thankful for someone to be there with us to explain things to him.

Our church didn't have a graveyard yet, so we had to decide where Chad would be buried. We had two choices, the town cemetery, or one that was more out in the country. We chose the latter.

Visitors from a distance started arriving on Saturday. Tim's parents came from Pennsylvania, and my parents from Virginia. Our families put forth much effort to be here for us. All of our brothers and sisters from both our families made it to the funeral. That included much traveling on their part. Three families came from Oregon, one from California, one from British Columbia, one from Ontario, two from Guatemala, one from North Carolina, one from Kentucky, and the rest from Pennsylvania and Virginia.

One thing that was especially hard for us to accept was the fact that the undertaker would not let us see the body until right before the viewing began on Sunday afternoon. Because of Chad's injuries, he wanted to make sure that he was fixed up just right and he didn't want us to see him until he was ready. We asked if we, as a family, could come in to the funeral home on Saturday to see him, but he didn't even want us to do that. It seemed like a long, long time from Thursday evening to Sunday afternoon, when we were finally allowed to view his body. The undertaker had done a very good job of fixing him up. He looked so sweet and peaceful lying there. We slept much better at night after being able to view Chad's body. Before that, every time we would close our eyes, we would see what he looked like at the time of the accident. We thought he looked like himself in the casket, although his head was swollen and he looked bigger than what he actually was.

The viewing was from 3:00 to 8:00 Sunday afternoon and evening. It was a comfort to us that others took the time to come. Then there was the question of what to do with the body overnight. We wanted to bring it home to our house, but didn't know what the undertaker would say about that. He said it would be all right. We will always be glad that we had that opportunity. It seemed like such a short time the way it was, from Sunday afternoon until the casket was closed for the last time following the funeral service on Monday. So we were glad for a little more time to view him. Duane Hoover transported the casket to our place and came at 8:00 Monday morning to take it to the church.

Many friends and relatives gathered that morning for the funeral. The service was very meaningful and comforting to us.

Many, many times during those first days we wondered how people ever make it through a time of trial such as this without God, and without Christian friends.

The burial took place at the Marion Cemetery several miles from the church. It was extremely cold and windy there, so after the grave side service was over, everyone quickly headed back to the church where lunch was served. Those who wanted to talk to us did so there where it was warmer.

It was sort of a relief to have the funeral over with. Yet we knew that there were going to be some hard days ahead.

Some of the family was able to stay for several days. Some visited other relatives in Wisconsin. My folks stayed until Friday morning. A different family was with us each day Tuesday through Friday that first week.

We felt so unworthy of all the things that others did for us in the next several months. The church people did so good at coming to visit us, bringing meals in, or just simply lending a listening ear when we needed it. The young folks made a tape for us that we highly treasure. They sang most of the songs that were sung at the funeral and grave side, plus some others as well. The church people also made a scrapbook for us which brought comfort to our bleeding hearts many times. Some remembered us by sending flower bouquets, and we received many cards and letters. Mail time was always a special time of the day for all of us.

One thing that we felt was perfectly timed by God was the gospel sign on our mailbox. These signs are a church project and are rotated monthly. This particular one was put in our sign frame a week or so before the accident, and it certainly did fit the occasion. On one side it said, *"God shall wipe away all tears."* On the other side it said, *"Lay up treasures in heaven"*.

Another thing that may seem minor to others, but to us seemed planned by God, was the fact that Chad was born on May 22, left his earthly home on March 22, and he was exactly 22 months old.

Although it is two years since Chad left us, we still miss him very much at times and can't help but wonder what it would be like if he would still be here. He was always such a cheerful little boy and the house was so quiet without him. He talked at a young age, and we feel like we have more memories of him because of that. When it was time to go to bed at night, he had never fussed, but would always be ready to crawl in and go to sleep. He liked to say his bedtime prayer, grab his teddy bear and hold it tight, then lay down and say, "See ya' in the morning," in his sweet baby voice. In the morning he would awaken with a big smile and say, "Good morning."

I remember telling the other children different times, "What would we ever do without our little Chaddy boy?" He brought so much sunshine to our home that we thought that we would never be able to make it without him. We are thankful for all the memories that we have of him. It is a comfort to know that he is much happier now than what he ever was here on earth.

Five months after Chad's death, our home was again

blessed with a sweet little baby, a girl whom we named Lavelle Arlene. No, she didn't take the place of Chad, but we were thankful to again have a baby in our home and in our arms. She has brought a lot of comfort to us.

We will never forget the blessing that Chad was to our home, and we thank God for lending him to us for twenty-two happy months.

Following is a writing that Carlos Witmer from our church wrote and gave to us the morning following the accident. It meant so much to us that we had it read at the funeral.

He Added A Flower To His Bouquet

On the evening of March 22, as Tim prepared to go outside with the children, his wife, Lois, called after him, "Take care of the children!"

Little did she realize the full meaning of those words, for the angels of heaven had heard and would fulfill the request at the command of the Lord. And little did Tim realize the role he was to play in fulfilling the call of God for little Chad.

As Tim stopped the tractor to allow the children to climb in, Chad heard someone call him. A voice only Chad was meant to hear called softly, "Chad, come Home."

A child of obedience, Chad looked around. There, not far away was Jesus, arms outstretched, smiling, a heavenly radiance on His face. "Come," He said, "COME HOME."

Chad knew who it was, and he stepped unnoticed from the bucket of the tractor to answer the call of Jesus, and the angels were waiting for Chad as the accident released his spirit from his body so he could fully answer the call of God. Tenderly they bore him to the loving arms of his Maker, and he recognized the face of the One who called him, as He said, "Welcome Home!"

God called and Chad answered. When God calls, man can but answer as Chad did.

God's purposes are not always fully or immediately revealed, and though we may never fully understand why, we know that God only takes the best.

Although Chad left his earthly family, we believe that Grandpa, Uncle Edward, and others were standing at the pearly gates waiting to welcome him home.

Although our hearts bleed, we will not question the timing or actions of our Almighty God, and we rejoice for Chad is still with family — and with Jesus!

—Carlos Witmer

—Tim & Lois Reinford
Redgranite, Wisconsin

LELAND EARL MARTIN

January 13, 1975 to January 4, 1985 (9 years)

God Is Love

Henry Martin, Father

On January 4, 1985, my wife and I had been on a business trip to Quincy, Illinois. One of our stops that day was at a rummage sale in Quincy. It was late when we got home, and the children had most of the chores done when we got back. The children had expected us to come home with toys and some things they were in need of. As I backed toward the house, Leland was right there motioning me how far to back up. I can still see him in the darkness, *"C'mon, Dad. C'mon, Mom."*

Later in the evening we got a phone call from my brother Willis' children. They wanted our boys to come ice skate with them. We decided they could go skating for an hour, then come home again. Knowing that twelve-year-old Merle was quite skillful with the tractor, I told them they should just take the tractor. After all, it was only one-and-one-half miles to Willis'. On the way over the tractor's front wheel caught a snowbank and pulled the tractor over right at a steep ditch.

The rear wheel of the tractor slipped into the ditch, rolling the tractor upside-down with our two sons underneath it. Merle crawled out from under it with barely a scratch, but Leland's head was pinned under the fender.

It took a while to get the tractor off Leland. When we got Leland free, we thought we felt a pulse. We tried CPR till the ambulance came and took him to the hospital.

Only those who have experienced such a time of intense anxiety can realize what we as parents were going through at that time. We prayed, "Lord, Thy will be done." I must say, amidst the turmoil, we could feel God's comforting hand.

At the hospital they put Leland on a ventilator. However, the doctor soon came and said, "The body is being kept alive, but the brain is dead." We, as parents, needed to decide if they should continue trying to sustain him. There was a slight chance to regain life, but Leland would probably be brain-damaged. Our minister and other family members were present. With their encouragement, we decided to let God have His way.

In looking back, we do not feel it was an accident. We feel it was planned. God had a lesson to teach us.

I had to deal with self-blame for a while. If only, if only — if only I would not have allowed them to go. Now seventeen years later, I can still see Leland motioning to me over yonder and saying, *"C'mon, Dad. C'mon, Mom."*

"Blessed be God, even the Father of our Lord Jesus Christ, the Father of mercies and the God of all comfort" (II Corinthians 1:3).

Jesus, while our hearts are bleeding
O'er the spoils that death has won,
We would, at this solemn meeting,
Calmly say,—Thy will be done.

Tho' cast down we're not forsaken;
Though afflicted, not alone;
Thou didst give, and Thou hast taken;
Blessed Lord—Thy will be done.

By Thy hands the boon was given;
Thou hast taken but Thine own;
Lord of earth, and God of Heaven,
Evermore,—Thy will be done.

—Song taken from *Mennonite Hymns*

—Henry & Ella Martin
Arbela, Missouri

John Wesley Fisher

November 15, 1997 to March 29, 2001 (3 years)

O Gentle One We Miss You Here

Wilma Fisher, Mother

The date was Thursday, March 29, 2001. It looked as if it would rain as we finished our morning chores. I came into the house to find our three little boys playing. (This scene is etched in my mind because it is the last time I would come into the house to three boys.) After breakfast we had our family devotions. It was five-year-old Wilson and three-year-old John Wesley's turn to pray. Normally John Wesley would have prayed for the cows and anything else he could think of, but this morning he only prayed for Daddy and Mama, Wilson and Seth, then said, "Amen." This prayer is very precious to me.

That morning Sam (Daddy) had talked about going to the other farm with the skid-loader to put out bales and remove some water from the barn. He had said only one boy could go along, so Wilson was planning to go. John Wesley cried because he wanted to go along too.

After devotions, Sam didn't feel like going out right away so he said he would read to us. I went into the laundry room, and there stood John Wesley all dressed to go out. I guess he wanted to make sure he didn't "miss my boat," as he liked to say. Sam then decided they might as well go and get the work done before it rained, and he could read when they got back. I helped the boys get their clothes zipped up. Sam had said the boys could both go after all. Little did I realize that I was zipping that little purple barn coat for the last time. I let them go out to play a little till Daddy was ready to go. A little later I looked out and saw the two boys walking around carrying sticks. Then they rolled on the ground, apparently fighting over them. I told Sam, "Surely, with all the trees we have, there's enough sticks for everyone."

A little while later I had looked out the kitchen window and saw my dear sons squatting at a drainage ditch "fishing" with their sticks. This was the last time I saw John Wesley alive.

They left with Daddy on the skid-loader a short time later.

I was working at the wash and doing some embroidery, while looking forward to an afternoon with my husband and sons. Around 10:00, the answering machine came on twice but the phone hadn't rung. (We later discovered that the phone battery was dead.) I got up and turned the machine off and had just sat back down when the doorbell rang. I thought it was Sam, as he did that sometimes. I happily went to the door only to find a stranger there. He told me, "Grab your coat and come with me. Your son has been in an accident." I tried to get some satisfaction out of him but he refused to give me any. He put me in his truck, as I could hardly walk from shock, and took me up the road to the accident site.

First I saw the skid-loader, then I saw a little boot. I knew before I saw John Wesley that it was him because I only had one little boy who lost his boots. I saw my precious son lying there covered with a blanket, all alone. My mind refused to believe what I was seeing. John Wesley had fallen over the back of the skid-loader bucket and his head had been driven over. Wilson had also been riding in the bucket. Sam said just before the accident the boys were so happy, laughing and talking together. He thought of John Wesley falling off and told him to move over, and that is when he fell.

I tried to talk to Sam who was crying and repeating over and over what he had done. But he was too hysterical to even notice me. I went over and sat by my beloved baby. He was bleeding and his eyes were open so I could hardly stand to look at him. But he was my child, and my heart went out to him as always before. I sat on the ground beside him and put my one arm around him. I held his chubby little hand in mine and put my fingers up under his coat sleeve where he was still so nice and warm. I rested my head on him and tried to pray, but I don't think my mind was clear enough to say much. I stayed with him till the medics came and told me I needed to move. They erected a tarp to form a tent from the mailbox, to where he was laying. I appreciated this because it had just started to rain as though the heavens were crying with us.

Someone loaned me their van and I took it back to the house to get one-year-old Seth whom I had left sleeping. Wilson, Seth, and I sat in the van and watched while the authorities did their business. The coroner finally came and took John Wesley's body to perform an autopsy, which is the law.

We were at the accident scene for about two hours. When we got back to the house, our minister and his wife were there. Many more friends and relatives came that day and in the following days. On Friday we went to the funeral home to make final arrangements and to deliver John Wesley's clothing. The undertaker did not have his body yet.

Sunday morning we traveled to Shafferstown for the afternoon and evening visitation. There was a private viewing for close friends and family prior to the visitation. But due to his injuries the casket remained closed after our viewing. He did not look like himself at all. So it still didn't fix in my mind that he was gone. I hoped it would.

We had the funeral at 10:00 Monday morning. Elvin Horst moderated and read some poems. I'm not positive in what order things were, but we had the following poems read during the service:

"Memories of John Wesley" written by his daddy, "The Children Up In Heaven," and a poem without a title that starts out: "Don't you worry Mother." We also sang the following songs: "Safe In The Arms Of Jesus," "Gathering Buds," "How Beautiful Heaven Must Be," and "Some Sweet Day." Warren Auker had devotions and Harlan Martin had the sermon. Joel Landis had the grave side service where he read the requested poem, "Angels Are Hard To Find." We also sang: "Only a Boy Named David," "Building Up The Temple" which were favorites of John Wesley's, and "Jesus Loves Me."

When they had asked about pall bearers, three boys came to my mind right away. These were teenage boys, but John Wesley had thought a lot of them. We had Sam's oldest nephew for the fourth one.

We miss our dear little boy so much. The void is just so hard to accept. The thought that was brought out at the funeral, "We know without a shadow of a doubt where John Wesley is," has been a comfort many times. It gives us "more to go to heaven for than we had yesterday." Sometimes my mind is like a broken record, continuously singing:

This World Is Not My Home

This world is not my home, I'm just a passing thru'
My treasures are laid up somewhere beyond the blue,
The angels beckon me from heaven's open door,
And I can't feel at home in this world anymore.

I have my dear John Wesley over in glory land.
I don't expect to stop until I take his hand.
He's waiting now for me by heaven's open door
And I can't feel at home in this world anymore.

Just over in glory land we'll live eternally,
The saints on every hand are shouting victory,
Their songs of sweetest praise ring back from heaven's shore
And I can't feel at home in this world anymore.

Oh Lord, you know I have no friend like you
If heaven's not my home then Lord what will I do
The angels beckon me from heaven's open door
And I can't feel at home in this world anymore.

—Rewritten by Wilma Fisher

~

One Year Later

March 29, 2002, — that can't be right! Has it already been a year since he left us to join that angel band? It seems like only yesterday that my precious son ran around the house, played with his brothers, and added spice with his childish sense of humor.

This time of year has been very hard. All month it was kind of like a countdown. One year ago he was still here for ten days, nine days, eight days, etc. This morning it almost seemed like we were reliving the last March 29, and that somehow I could prevent the accident.

It is only by the grace of God and the kindness of friends, family, and our church at Port Royal that has brought us to, and helped us through, this day.

One year ago at the scene of the accident the ambulance driver had put her arm around me and told me how sorry she was. I said, "He's in heaven. What more could we want?" The truth had not really sunk in yet. Little did I know the pain, grief, and sorrow that would come with learning to live without my little son.

I really disliked the saying, "In acceptance lieth peace." I felt like I had accepted but still I could not find peace. Almost eight months after John Wesley's death I finally found true peace. During a week of revivals the speaker spoke on heaven, describing how beautiful heaven was! I finally was able to see it as a real place, the place were my son lives!

However, lately it seems I've had to fight some of the same battles again that I had fought before, and thought I had won.

Eight months after John Wesley left us, another small son was added to our family. This was a little hard to accept since he will never know his brother, and John Wesley really loved babies. We named our baby Jarin in memory of his brother's name, and for our hired boy, Jared. I can still hear him saying on his toy cell phone, "Thank you, Jarin." (That is how John Wesley said *Jared*.)

We have made many new friends through losing our son, especially other parents who have lost children.

Our daily prayer continues to be that the Lord would return soon, and in the meantime may our eyes and hearts never be drawn to the things on this earth again.

—Sam & Wilma Fisher
Gettysburg, Pennsylvania

Memories of John Wesley

John Wesley dear, you're gone, you're gone,
Oh what a dreadful fate,
But wait, you're in glory land,
Singing with the angel band;
With Uncle Elam gone before,
There on the golden shore.

John Wesley, oh John Wesley dear,
How you are missed by us.
Oh we would like to cuddle you
And squeeze your little hand,
For you were sweet and cuddlesome,
And full of mischief too!

You still knew how to touch our hearts
As only you could do.

John Wesley, oh John Wesley dear,
Oh, how sweet you were
Just before you left this earth;
Riding in the skid loader bucket with big brother Wilson,
Looked to Daddy like you were having a great time.
Then Daddy thought of the danger of his little lad
Riding too close to the edge!
With that in mind, came Daddy's words, "Move over," but alas!
What Daddy feared would happen, quickly came to pass!

Oh John Wesley dear, my son, my son,
My own beloved son,
Scuffed up and bruised and driven over
Oh is there any life in you at all?
With hope Daddy picked you up and carried you a little way
And laid you on the grass.
So after mouth to mouth
Oh how terrible, Daddy gave in to death's claim.

So now, John Wesley, oh John Wesley dear,
We commit you to God who gave you to us.
Oh it is hard to give you up,
But now we can trust you to Jesus' loving arms!
So good-bye John Wesley, oh John Wesley dear
Good night, John Wesley! Sleep tight, sleep tight!

Hugs and Kisses, Family and All
—Sam Fisher, Father

Beryl Martin

July 14, 1987 to May 30, 1992 (4 years)

Christin Martin

August 23, 1991 to February 9, 1993 (17 months)

Stephen Martin

February 14, 1976 to January 20, 1999 (22 years)

Three Angels

Lydia Martin, Single Mother of foster & adopted children

I am a single foster and adoptive parent having first adopted son Stephen in August of 1977 at the age of eighteen months. In December of 1982 I received my first foster child, and am still doing foster care. In September of 1983 I adopted my daughter Jolene.

In March of 1988 I received a seven-month-old baby girl into my home by the name of Beryl. Beryl was diagnosed with Canavans Syndrome, a fatal diagnosis. Her mother walked out of the hospital, and out of her daughter's life after being told of the diagnosis. Her father could not care for her, but didn't want to give her up for adoption, so I took her in under temporary custody agreement. Beryl had many ups and downs but at four years of age was doing the best she had ever done, looking so good, and how we all enjoyed and loved her. In January of 1992 when Beryl was four-and-one-half years old, she started with seizures. She laid unresponsive in the hospital for three days. I feared we would lose her then but she bounced back to the same sweetheart we had known. We were so happy. A few weeks later, I took her back to the doctor and received another blow. Her eyes were not focusing anymore and they wanted to do an MRI. This did not reveal the problem, and Beryl's health continued to decline. She was vomiting frequently. On May 5, she was admitted to the hospital. Many tests were done, but everyone was baffled — and Beryl continued her decline. On May 18, she finally had an MRI with contrast. At 8:00 that evening the neurosurgeon took me into a room, showed me her x-rays, and said, "Beryl has a Brainstem tumor, it is cancerous, and has spread." Words cannot describe my shock — first a syndrome, and now a tumor! She had a shunt installed, and another surgery to relieve the pressure. But on May 30, Beryl lost her battle for life on this earth.

A beautiful flower too precious to stay,
God in His mercy took her away...
Not from our memory... not from our love,
But to be an Angel in Heaven above.

I struggled on in my deep grief and eventually listened

to the needs of some other children who needed a home. I was asked to take a little boy who needed a kidney transplant, or else a one-year-old baby girl who had been born prematurely and had lots of problems. It was hard to decide which one to take, but my social worker said, "We don't want to place one with a fatal diagnosis in her care. She just lost a little girl."

I did take Christin into my home in August of 1992, three months after Beryl's death. Christin had many hospital stays, surgeries, etc., but after five months of hard work she was really looking good, had I known! On February 2, 1993, I placed Christin in a respite home because I was going to the hospital for surgery. Christin looked so good when I left her there.

One week later on February 9, with me lying on the couch in a lot of pain, I had a knock on my door. My social worker was at the door unannounced. I was told to sit down, and was given the shocking news that my baby was found dead in the crib that morning! The tears just flowed — there were no proper words. I muddled through this funeral in great pain, physically and emotionally. I just did this eight months ago! The doctors told me she had pneumonia in one lung but that should not have killed her.

So much for social workers to decide which child will live and which will die. These are God's children and only loaned to us. Christin was buried in a Philadelphia cemetery on a beautiful, snowy February day — beautiful like she was.

Again life went on. I felt like I didn't do anything but cry for about two years. Each part of the years brought some special reminder back of my girls. I was very busy over the next years, often having six special-needs children in my home at a time.

In December of 1998, Stephen started crying out in his sleep at times, and he was also having seizures. We changed and increased his seizure medications, but despite all this he became worse. Stephen started to fall a lot, and I noticed his eyes were not focusing! I took him to the emergency room a few times, but to no avail. Finally, on January 7 we took him to an eye doctor. That doctor was very much alarmed and sent us to an eye specialist. She set up a very extensive MRI to be done on January 11. In the meantime, Stephen was really suffering and declining in health. At 4:00 that Monday afternoon I again got the shocking news that another one of my children had a brain tumor. Stephen had a very large malignant tumor in his R. frontal lobe. That was the same lobe of his brain where he had a blood clot as a newborn baby. (The doctors said the two conditions were not related.)

Stephen was admitted to the hospital overnight, which I've always regretted. I talked to many doctors, but was given no hope for healing. I finally said, "Then why would we pursue any surgeries, etc.? He is suffering enough." They finally arranged with Hospice to have him brought home the next day.

Stephen declined more every day and suffered tremendously. Jesus finally took him home on January 20.

Again I just cried — trying to make sense out of life. Slowly Jesus helped heal my bleeding heart. With time more foster children left my home, some going to very bad situations. I was finally able to be thankful that at least these three are not suffering. There are certainly a lot worse things than death when we are prepared to meet our Savior — my three angels were prepared!

—Lydia Martin
Ephrata, Pennsylvania

NOLAN DURRELL LAUVER

June 15, 1996 to October 1, 1998 (2 years)

A Tug From Heaven's Anchor

Edith Lauver, Mother

The last day of September we made plans to go to our bishop's mother-in-law's viewing. Anticipating a big crowd, we decided to try to get there about the time it started. There were a nice amount of people there already when we arrived but the line was steadily moving. As we were walking toward the casket the thought passed through my mind, *"I wonder when it will be our turn to stand in line, like this family, receiving condolences."* We chatted with a few friends then went home. Two-year-old Nolan fell asleep on the way home. I carried him into the house and laid him on our bed intending to only let him sleep an hour.

When the children came home from school, we soon got at the milking and evening chores. About 6:00, I suddenly thought about Nolan. He was still sleeping. I had not meant to let him sleep so long but it had slipped my mind so I awakened him right away.

After the supper dishes and homework were done, we all pulled up chairs in the living room for devotions. As a two-year-old, Nolan didn't always like to sit nicely for devotions but this evening he climbed up on a chair and looked up at his daddy with a big smile seeming to say, *"See Daddy. I can be nice."* We sang ten or twelve songs that evening, whereas we usually sing only five or six. One song we sang was "Jesus loves all the children, 1-2-3 children, 4-5-6 children, 7-8-9 children..." I commented then how well that song fit our family of nine children, and how thankful I was for each one of them. I also said how I hoped each one would grow up to serve the Lord and be faithful all their lives. The thought came to me as I looked around at each face. *"How precious these children are! How good God has been to give us such a precious family! I wonder how long we'll all be together like this."* I was thinking more along the line that our oldest daughter would be 16 years old in a few days and what changes the next couple of years could hold.

Nolan sat nicely the whole time during devotions, glancing at me every now and then with a big smile. When we were going to bed, Jason said, "Maybe we're finally getting through to Nolan," thinking of all our efforts in disciplining him. Nolan had been a tough one to teach and we often felt discouraged as it seemed many times it was two steps forward and one backward in getting him to learn obedience and submission. He was a sweet, happy boy, but sometimes I felt other people didn't see that side of him. Jason, in sensing his fatherly responsibility, prayed that night that the Lord would help him to help Nolan into heaven.

Everyone got settled for the night but because of Nolan's

late nap he wasn't tired. I let him climb into the girl's bed so Jason could sleep while I got four-month-old Janelle settled. Then I went for Nolan, but he had already fallen asleep. I was glad. I picked him up to put him in his bed but as soon as I laid him down he sat right back up. I tried to get him to lay down for a while, but he just wasn't very tired. So I sat in the rocking chair and held him while rocking. Even if he wasn't tired, I was. I must have dozed off because I awoke at around 12:30 a.m. and here I was still holding Nolan. How warm and cuddly he felt against me — *"Such a sweet little boy,"* I thought, as the night-light fell across his innocent face. I carried him to his bed and he slept the rest of the night, uneventfully. Looking back, I feel it was a very precious gift from God to allow me to hold Nolan for several hours during his last night on earth.

The next morning it was the usual rush of getting six children ready and off to school. Jason read some stories to Matthew and Nolan while I took the children to school. When I came back, he and I and the preschoolers ate breakfast. Nolan didn't want to eat nicely so Jason gave him a few swats and told him to sit up like a big boy and eat nicely, and he did.

After breakfast Jason went outside to work and I worked around the house. Janelle played on the floor. Matthew and Nolan were soon wanting to go outside too. I told Nolan to help pick up a game first. When we were done he looked at me with a big smile and said, "All done!" Those are the last words I remember him saying.

Before I realized it Nolan ran outside with bare feet and no coat. (This October morning was too cold for bare feet.) I hurriedly scooped him up, brought him back inside, set him on the wash machine, and washed his feet. He giggled as I tickled his "piggies". After his socks and shoes were on, and his jacket zipped up, he went outside to play while I put Janelle to sleep for her morning nap.

I could see the boys outside the living room window playing like they were mixing feed for the cows. The leaves were silage, the grass was haylage, and the dirt minerals.

When I had Janelle sleeping I went out to pick lima beans. The boys followed me to the garden. Matthew turned on the hose to make dams and lakes. I didn't think that was a very good idea as I didn't want them to get wet. So he turned the water off and they played in the dirt close by me. Nolan soon came over to where I was picking and was looking for beans to pick too. I showed him some he could pick. He was pleased. He would pick a bean and look up at me and smile. I remember thinking, *"What a sweet little boy."*

I finished picking beans and got a shovel to dig the sweet potatoes. I called the boys to come and pick them up for me and lay them out on top of the ground to dry. As they were picking them up Matthew chattered all the while about all the funny shapes. Nolan was tramping on some, breaking them. I could hear Jason pounding on the chopper in the nearby field. I mentioned to the boys about Daddy fixing the chopper. Nolan lost interest after a while and walked across the yard toward the sandbox. Matthew stayed with me picking up sweet potatoes. I was wondering how long Janelle would sleep and was anxious to get my job done. I finished digging and went into the house to check on Janelle. I didn't hear her stirring so I thought I would run and get the mail quick yet, as we were looking for the milk check that day.

While I was at the mailbox, a cattle truck came down the road and turned in. He stopped at the mailbox and asked if this is where the dead cow was. (A dry cow had died the day before.) I told him he had the right place, and he asked where she was lying. I pointed behind the barn, and in doing so I saw the cows were out. I wondered how they could be out because Jason was not working in that area. I ran quickly to round them up because we live along a very busy road and we are always careful about not letting cows get on the road. I saw Jason coming from the opposite direction and thought, *"Good, I won't have to get them in by myself."* I ran around the shop to head them off. While I was still running, I heard Jason give a terrible cry of anguish — like I never heard before. I ran faster and hollered, *"What's wrong?"* Then I saw him coming with Nolan, limp and bluish-gray, in his arms. *"He's gone!"* Jason cried in disbelief. "I'm sure he's gone!" I jumped across the cable which was attached to the dead cow, and the thought, *"Safe in the arms of Jesus,"* flashed through my mind. Jason laid him on the gravel but I picked him up again. Matthew had heard the commotion and came too. He tugged on my skirt, saying "He's just sleeping." "No, Matthew," I said, "Nolan is with Jesus."

I remember thinking, *"My little boy is dead and I'm not crying. What's wrong with me? These men probably think I should be crying."* I laid Nolan on the grass then ran to the phone and dialed 911. Then I hung up before they answered, thinking, *"Well, he's dead. Why call the ambulance?"* And I couldn't call our ministry because I knew they were at Katherine Miller's funeral. The phone rang almost immediately after I hung up. It was 911 calling back, asking if I had called. I said, "Yes, we think our little boy was killed." I gave our name and brief directions, then hung up. I was shaking and wanted to go back to Nolan. They called again, and this time Jason picked it up. They asked if anyone was doing CPR. I could have screamed. *"Why didn't I think of it?!"* By now several more minutes had passed, *"Why didn't I thump him right away and breathe into him?"* I ran to him again and pinched his nose shut and breathed into him. His chest rose and fell but the air just gurgled out of him. I was aware that he was feeling cold around his mouth. I took his shoes off and lifted his shirt. I could see a deep compression mark on his chest and near his throat where the gate had rested on him.

Apparently he was looking for his daddy and had crawled through the barnyard gate. Then he could see around a few rows of standing corn and noticed his daddy was in the field instead. In trying to come back through the gate he must have pulled it off the block, and as it goes down a little grade, it knocked him off his feet and the gate came up across his body, resting heavily on his chest and throat. The clip on the chain to hold the gate shut was broken. We had temporarily pinched a block of wood between the gate and the post, never thinking of it as a death trap.

When the ambulance arrived, the crew worked on Nolan. I kept asking if they were getting a pulse but they wouldn't answer me. I read their clipboard upside-down: *Confirmed cardiac arrest upon arrival.* So I was assured that they knew he was gone, but just wouldn't tell us. One paramedic questioned Matthew as to what he knew about what had happened. Jason showed several policemen how and where it had happened.

After they put Nolan into the ambulance, Jason and I quickly changed our clothes and picked the baby out of bed. I called my mother, also Ruby Mack and asked her to contact the ministry. One policeman asked us if we were able to drive by ourselves. Jason said he thought so. I saw Nolan's little pile of clothing on the bank as we were leaving and I thought, *"How will I ever be able to pick them up when we get home?"* A neighbor lady had come when she saw the ambulance at our place. She took Matthew along home with her.

When we arrived at the hospital, we were met at the door by a chaplain who asked us our names and ushered us into a room for prayer. I knew then that it was final. He waited with us a little while, then some doctors came in and sat down. With a sober face, one said, "We're sorry — he's gone. We did all we could." I said, "We knew he was." We all sat there in silence a while. What was there to say? I asked them if we could go to Nolan and they took us to him.

How sweet and precious he looked! He had a little dirt on his forehead and also his hand. How I wished I could use a wash cloth on him and take him home to eat dinner with us. I stroked his hair and kissed his cold forehead. This was my baby boy! How could I let him go? All the work and effort we had put into his life, and now he was gone! We couldn't comprehend yet what "gone forever" meant. I lifted the sheet and saw Nolan still had his socks on. I sadly pulled them off and put them in my purse. The curtain parted and Mark and Naomi Rosenberry walked in, shook hands, and offered their heartfelt sympathy. In some ways I felt cold and stiff and hardly able to cry. We briefly told them the story.

Then we were asked to go into a room to talk to the coroner and a policeman. The policeman questioned us. At one point I said, "I know I should have checked on him sooner, but I was trying to hurry up and finish because I was afraid the baby would be crying." The policeman said, "We're not trying to get you in a corner, Mrs. Lauver. We know you can't watch your children every minute of the day. You raised several others didn't you?" How consoling those words were! What relief washed down over me as I realized they were not blaming us! The coroner wanted permission to do an autopsy, and wondered about organ donation. We decided against organ donation. As for the autopsy, we didn't want it. But they said because there were no petechiae (little broken blood vessels) in his eyes or on his face as usually accompanies a suffocation death, they needed to verify the cause of Nolan's death. We reluctantly gave our consent.

Then we discussed with Marks about bringing the children home from school and telling them the shocking news. We wanted to bring the children to the hospital to see Nolan before they took him for the autopsy. Mark made several phone calls to those that knew something had happened to confirm that Nolan really was gone. It struck me that the whole emergency room was deathly quiet. It seemed that everyone was watching to see how we would react.

Marks went to school to get our children while we went home. When we walked in the door, there were Joel and Cheryl Martin who came to share our grief and help with the chores. My mother and niece were also there. Marks came with the school children and we gathered in the living room where Jason told them the sad news. We all cried together. Then we went to the hospital to see little Nolan. We could hardly get done looking at him. We pulled ourselves away. Was this really happening? Our poor little boy!

Back home again, Jason gave some instructions to the "Good Samaritans" who were doing our chores. The sad news had spread at Katherine Miller's grave side, so several people came to see whether they could help in any way or just to extend their sympathy.

That evening the ministry, grandparents, and others came to help make funeral plans. The undertaker also came. We planned to have the viewing on Sunday and the funeral on Monday, October 5.

There was little sleep for Jason and I that night. We talked and cried for hours. The next morning we went to the church graveyard to pick out a grave site. That afternoon we took clothes to the funeral home for Nolan. We asked the funeral director if we could dress him and he consented. Jason and I dressed him — oh, the heart pangs — for the very last time! The undertaker brought a cup of water and a comb and I combed his hair. How sweet he looked — my little man!

Back home again, there was a group of men refilling our silo and doing other jobs. In the house my mother and sisters-in-law were polishing shoes and trying to get clothes ready for the coming days. We felt overwhelmed by everyone's thoughtfulness.

One disgusting thing that happened was the TV reporter that stopped in to take pictures. Of course, they did not have permission to take pictures and were trying to take them on the wrong side of the barn. My brother Ethan told them firmly that the Mother of the child specifically requests that no coverage be given. It took a lot of insisting, but they finally left us alone. That night we were so exhausted, but slept only two hours.

Saturday we went to the funeral home again. I regretfully knew we had no family picture of all nine of our children, so we took one of all the children around their little brother's casket.

Sunday morning the undertaker brought Nolan out to the house for a few hours. It was a very special time. Our parents and other close family members came to be with us. We sang several songs and read a passage of Scripture. The Sunday school lesson was on Hannah lending Samuel to the Lord. We also had lent our little boy to the Lord.

The viewing was a large one with over 1200 people filing through. We felt overwhelmed by so many people showing their love and sympathy. I dreaded the thought of the funeral the next day. *How could I bear to bury my little boy out of sight? What if I cried uncontrollably?*

The day of the funeral dawned chilly and drizzly. Words cannot describe all my feelings that day. *How is a mother to bury her baby son? How can you describe the heavy ache in your heart when the casket lid is closed for the last time, shutting out his baby face forever from your view? How can a mother allow them to shovel the grave shut over her little son?* What a blessing is our faith and the hope of heaven at such a time! What a comfort were all our friends and relatives. We were told there were about 425 people at the funeral.

Tuesday, the day after the funeral, was a hard day. No one came and we were exhausted physically and emotionally. *How can one measure the tears that fell? How can one tell of the empty spot in the family*? Now Jason had no little boy to hold in church anymore. Matthew and Janelle were a great source of comfort to all of us. Matthew talked and talked about Nolan, and Janelle was a sweet, cuddly baby to love.

One day Matthew pretended to talk to Nolan on the phone asking when he was coming back to play with him. "When you get done sleeping, come play with me." "Well, I won't get done sleeping for a long time." "When you *do* get done sleeping, come play with me." "I'll be sleeping for a long, long time." Matthew missed his playmate so much.

Another time when he was washing dishes, he called Nolan's name over and over. Once he said, "I wish Elijah (meaning Elisha) was here. Then he could make our little boy get alive again, like that other little boy." On another occasion he asked, "If we'd have been back of the barn when Nolan's heart went up to Jesus, could we have seen it go?"

One day when it seemed everyone else had something to do but him, he blurted out, "Go get Nolan so I have somebody to play with!" He would beg me to read some of the poems people sent every day for a long time. They seemed to give him as much comfort as me. For devotions he almost always picked "I Love the Think of My Home Above".

At school when the children had assignments of writing a poem or story for English or Reading, they would often write about Nolan. The girls, especially, expressed themselves on paper which was meaningful to me.

We had some unkind or unfair comments to deal with. Because our emotions were so raw, and our hearts ached with grief, those comments hurt more than usual. Some people thought we were careless in not having the clip fixed on the gate, but there will always be things to fix on a farm. We felt God's sovereign hand was over all and know He could have directed Nolan's steps otherwise. I never felt Jason was careless because I knew he worked hard to keep after things. He told me several months later that he had actually got up on the gate and jumped on it that morning to be sure the block was tight. That statement brought much comfort to me.

I really appreciate when people talk about Nolan, or tell us things that they remember about him. Sometimes when we mention something about Nolan to people, we are met with silence. That is very painful. People do not realize the very deep need to talk about it or to give us a chance to talk. It is so healing to tell the story again and again and to feel that maybe someone else misses him too.

We can honestly say we are very grateful for the added depth this experience has added to our life. We would not have asked for such a trial, but now we wouldn't want to be without all we have learned.

Sweet little flower too tender to stay,
God in His mercy took Nolan away.
Not from our memory, not from our love,
But to dwell with Him in heaven above.

—Jason & Edith Lauver
Shippensburg, Pennsylvania

In the suburb of a city
In a place we little crave
In a spot that's not much noticed
Lies a very little grave.

Just a little bud of promise
Just a precious bit of joy
But he vanished like a vapor
Gone! A lovely little boy.

Gone from earth, yes, gone forever,
Gone to bloom in Heaven above
Never seeing sin nor sorrow
Never knowing aught but love.

Why, we cannot tell the reason
Others have their joys complete
But it brings to mind a story
Which I willingly repeat.

'Twas a Shepherd in the country
Coming with His sheep one day
He had tried but could not get them
O'er the stream which crossed the way.

He had tried in every manner
All His efforts seemed in vain
When another thought had struck Him,
I will try just once again.

Down He stooped and raised a lambkin
'Twas the baby of the flock-
Bore it safely o'er the water
Ah, this time they didn't mock.

For the mother quickly followed
One by one the others came
And the Shepherd, He was happy
For His work was not I vain.

I am sure you see the picture
In my little story true,
For the sheep are like us people,
Ah, the sheep are just like you.

And the lamb, the darling baby,
Oh, he was your hope and pride
God, the Shepherd, bore it over
Safely to the other side.

He would have you trust in Jesus,
May His work be not in vain
He would have you meet your baby
At His coming back again.

—Poet Unknown

Contributors